The Golden Age of
HULL

The Golden Age of
HULL

Old Home Week, Neighbors and Gala Days

JOHN GALLUZZO

THE
History
PRESS

Published by The History Press
Charleston, SC 29403
www.historypress.net

Front Cover: The Old Ring, Hull's political machine, enjoyed the Golden Age of Hull more than anybody. Shown here, among others, are John L. Mitchell and James Jeffrey in the front row, and Boss John Smith, with the high white collar in the background between them.

Back Cover: The death of Police Chief, Fire Chief and Chairman of the Board of Selectmen Henry J. Stevens, in front at the left, caused a rift in town government. William Armour, standing in the front row to his right, took over as police chief.

All images courtesy of Hull Historical Society unless otherwise noted.

First published 2006

Manufactured in the United States

ISBN 1.59629.108.9

Library of Congress CIP data applied for.

Dedicated to Michelle.
At last.

Contents

Contents

Acknowledgements

Old Home Week brings me right back to the beginning of my professional writing life, and the first article for which I ever received a check, on David Porter Mathews. I owe a debt of gratitude to Bill and Helen Weiser for sharing their discovery with the people of Hull, Mathews for his thirst for the spotlight and, especially, to Susan Ovans and Roger Jackson for giving me a chance to write for the *Hull Times*. In fact, most of the writing that appears in *The Golden Age of Hull* first appeared in the *Hull Times*. As such, I cannot thank Roger and Susan enough.

So many other names pop up when I think of this book: the "No Place for Hate" committee, who asked me to think about Hull's diversity for a piece in the *Times*; Janet Bennett, our wonderful town clerk, who steered me to the right documents when I was in search of the origins of street names; Daniel Johnson and the staff at the Hull Public Library, especially Anne Bradford, Ann Rogers, Bea Kelly and Marlene Flattich, my secret weapon in the fight against the smothering sands of time; and Cap'n Bob Dever, who's always ready to share a story or two about Hull's past while dangling a few worms to their deaths in Boston Harbor.

The members of the Committee for the Preservation of Hull History—Chris Haraden, Rick Shaner, Jim Lampke, Regina Burke, Janet Jordan, Peter Seitz, Myron Klayman, Midge Lawlor and our recently departed friend and comrade Brison Shipley, the twenty-first century version of the "Old Ring"—have either suggested ideas, pointed out sources, or somehow aided in my work over the years. Richard Cleverly, the first recognized Hull History Hero, stands alone in the word of Hull history.

The crew at Fort Revere Park & Preservation Society, many named above, but in addition Fred Hills, Graeme Marsden, Sarah O'Loughlin, Susan Oberg, Harvey Jacobvitz, Sandy Bloom and Matt Tobin, have been a joy to work with over the years. Judeth Van Hamm, the grand creator of Hull's non-profit historical family, is always an inspiration as well.

The joy of writing a book is nothing without the support of family and friends. So Mom, Dad, Julie and Nick, thanks for being there. Thank you, too, David, Kathy and Matthew.

And, at last, I have a new family of my own. Thank you to beautiful Michelle, my wife, for sharing dreams, and not closing doors.

Any mistakes in this book are mine and mine alone. Blame me, not anyone else.

Introduction

Almost a decade ago, in May 1997, the *Hull Times* ran an article about a local couple, the ubiquitous Bill and Helen Weiser of Main Street, finding a notebook shoved behind the rafters in their attic while doing some remodeling. The notebook, they said, was full of poems by a guy named David Porter Mathews, but they really had no other information about him than his name. I read the article with interest, as I *knew* David Porter Mathews, or at least knew him in the historical sense. I had started doing some research for the Hull Lifesaving Museum that winter in preparation for the upcoming centennial anniversary of the Portland Gale of 1898. I had been reading roll after roll of microfilm, the old *Hull Beacon* weekly newspaper, and Mathews happened to be the managing editor of the paper that year, not to mention a nephew of lifesaver Joshua James. But then again, in small-town Hull, population four hundred, who wasn't?

I bumbled into the *Hull Times* office and told editor Susan Ovans, who knew me as "Marylou's son," that I had a history degree and could maybe write something about D.P. Mathews for her. She gave me some guidelines and a deadline and sent me on my way.

That was some 250 articles ago, and *The Golden Age of Hull* is the twentieth book I've authored or coauthored. All because David Porter Mathews, an unabashed self-promoter, wanted to be remembered through the ages, and so lodged his book of poetry in the attic on Main Street to be found by future generations.

Mathews, though, while a major influence in my research and writing life, is a small player in the story of this book. The subtitle, *Old Home Week*,

Neighbors and Gala Days, holds special significance. The first Old Home Week held in Hull in 1903 had both nationalistic and anti-immigration overtones, in a time when the "old" families of America were feeling threatened and displaced by the arrival of so many new faces, languages and customs. But the main stated purpose of the Old Home Week phenomenon was to hopefully reverse the flow of the diaspora of American youths from small towns into big cities; it was an attempt to help them reconfirm their roots, and let them see that while, yes, city life could be exciting, their hometown wasn't really that bad a place to be.

All around town, historic markers indicated sites that were of importance to the people of 1903. How many people from Hull today know that S.F. Smith, who wrote the lyrics and music for "America," once spent time in town? Who knows where the oldest dock in town was (hint: it still shows up at low tide)? Parades marched through the streets, historians made speeches about the community's past and athletic events drew spectators like never before.

That was Old Home Week the event. The book attempts to recreate that feeling of nostalgia. Through these pages you'll find stories of people you never knew lived in town, and of places that once held more significance than they do today. You'll better understand the names of some streets, will wonder at what a trip on a Hull-to-Boston steamer was like and will wish, at least momentarily, that time travel was possible. Each chapter will act as one of those historical markers of old, marking a place where and a time when something significant happened in the history of Hull.

While you read this book, please keep one question in mind: what's in your attic? I'd really like to know.

A Notebook in an Attic

From the editor [of the Hull Times*]: The Times' April 26 [1997] edition carried an article about a Hull couple, Helen and Bill Weiser, who found an old notebook filled with poems while renovating their attic.*

The poems were written by David Porter Mathews, of whom the Weisers knew little.

Enter John Galluzzo, a research associate at the Hull Lifesaving Museum, who knows a great deal out the poet and shares some of Mathews's history in the article that follows…

In 1928, Elroy S. Thompson wrote in his *History of Plymouth, Norfolk and Barnstable Counties*, "Go to Hull—here the sympathetic cooperation of the linotyper and proofreader is fervently solicited—and here you will find the greatest little town which makes the most noise for its size, has the oddest history…"

Perhaps the loudest voice of all those extolling the virtues of that "greatest little town" in the late 1890s belonged to the one-time editor of the *Hull Beacon*, David Porter Mathews.

D.P. Mathews was born on April 11, 1854, the son of a New Hampshire carpenter, Gideon Mathews, and his wife Catherine James, the older sister of local lifesaving hero, Captain Joshua James.

Like many children of his time, David bore the name of a public figure. His parents—like those of Hull's Osceola James, Daniel Webster Cleverly, Ambrose Burnside Mitchell, etc.—named their son for a well-known personality, in this case Admiral David Porter, a naval officer born in Boston

The Hull Village that David Porter Mathews knew was one centered around "Elm Square."

in 1790. As commander of the thirty-two-gun frigate *Essex*, Porter raided English commerce during the War of 1812. Porter's son, David Dixon Porter, also gained fame as a naval officer, as did the elder Porter's adopted son, David Glasgow Farragut.

As a young boy, David Porter Mathews found himself exposed to many things that would later strongly influence his life. From a diary kept by a boarder at Moses Tower's Nantascot House in 1862 comes this entry, dated September 13: "Gid Mathews on a bender, whether from his own supplies, old William's or young William's [James] rather uncertain…To post office—great crowd—Gid singing." And again on October 1: "Gid, our neighbor, in a terrific condition last night, singing strongly, liquor probably from next house to ours, Wm. James, the Second."

Gideon Mathews died on September 21, 1867, at age fifty-six. As early as 1882, his son David was giving temperance lectures at Hull's Methodist-Episcopal Church.

Mathews would become a prolific writer. Together with flamboyant and opinionated Floretta Vining, part busybody, part social activist,

As a young man, David Porter Mathews lectured on temperance at the Hull Methodist-Episcopalian Church.

Mathews would construct the Vining & Mathews Syndicate of South Shore Newspapers, which included the *Hull Beacon, Nantasket Breeze, Hingham Bucket, Cohasset Sentinel, Scituate Light, Marshfield Outlook, Duxbury Standard, Pembroke Citizen* and *Norwell Homestead*.

Some of the newspapers were original endeavors, while others, such as the *Breeze*, were older projects simply absorbed into the syndicate. Mathews also held the position of *Boston Globe* correspondent for Hull for several years.

He wrote with ego and he wrote with swagger. He loved to keep his name in the newspapers, whether by printing his own serial mystery ("The Man with the Dual Identity"), letting readers know of his relation to the famous captains Samuel and Joshua James, or exclaiming his own acts of bravado.

Amidst the swirling winds and deadly surf of the Portland Gale of 1898, he walked from Hull Village to the trains at Cohasset to make sure the

Globe would get its story. At the height of the storm he found refuge in a Massachusetts Humane Society hut, where he spent the night "without supper," according to the December 3, 1898 edition of the *Hull Beacon.*

On another occasion, when nervous townspeople spread the rumor that the infamous Chicago kidnapper Pat Crowe was in town, all the children were pulled off the streets, but the January 18, 1901 *Hull Beacon* reported that "David Porter Mathews roamed Broadway in Hull, notebook in hand. But Mr. Crowe did not molest him…"

Mathews's association with Floretta Vining would not last long. In an editorial in the *Beacon* of July 26, 1901, Vining explained, "These papers are run for business success. Advertisements from a legitimate business were received and Mr. Mathews did not care to continue under those circumstances…"

While Mathews spent time away from work at the newspaper syndicate for a few months due to illness, Vining took advantage of the opportunity to solicit liquor advertising for the first time. Mathews, sticking to his temperance guns, gracefully bowed out of the business. By September he had written two plays, both on the evils of drink, to be performed locally.

When not writing plays or newspaper columns, Mathews entertained himself as manager of the Hull Volunteer Lifesavers Band, penning excessively wordy missives for the town of Hull's annual reports as part of his duties as the sealer of weights and measures and spending time with his young family. He married a young woman named Carrie Alice Tenney, a Chelsea native, in the 1870s, and together they raised Catherine Mary (Kitty May), born in 1878; Eva, 1886; Mildred, 1888; Harold Lovell, 1893; and lost a stillborn child in Ruth in 1897. The 1898 obituary of David's mother, Catherine James Mathews, mentions four surviving granddaughters; perhaps others had been born in Boston, where the couple had lived prior to their time in Hull.

David Porter Mathews is just one of the many colorful characters from Hull's past. Thankfully, due to his constant presence in the *Hull Beacon,* and his obvious desire to be remembered (planting the notebook in the attic of 2 Main Street), his story is one that will not be lost to us. His story makes up one small piece of the lore of Hull, that town with the "oddest history…"

Neighbors

There once existed a time when sportsmen, like statesman and orator Daniel Webster of Marshfield, escaped the tedious mental strain of American political life and relaxed by wandering the open plains of the Hull peninsula. According to Professor John Moore's 1900 *History of Hull*, Webster "took great delight in visiting the beach for pleasure and relaxation. He often rambled with his gun in search of game. At night he would rest at the inn in Hull [the Sportsman, or Worrick's Inn]. There it is said he wrote out speeches."

A little over a half century later, Moore reported that duck hunting, on the land side anyway, had become a pastime of the past, as the discovery of Nantasket Beach as a potential summer resort led to the settlement of hitherto unpopulated stretches of the peninsula. "At the present day the change is so great that he [Webster] could not enjoy the privilege in this respect as he did then."

Hull's original settlers chose their site wisely. Nature's worst winter storms would have to battle hills to the northeast and southwest of Hull Village to inflict their intended damage. The site also provided access to a protected harbor for safe stowage of boats and a natural spring of fresh water. Even with all of these advantages, the settlement remained miniscule for more than two hundred years.

Tucked at the end of the peninsula, the people of Hull formed their own micro-culture, odd enough to outsiders to be described as living in a "Moon village at the end of the earth." To this day, Hull townies must bear accusations that their ancestors lured sailors to their deaths as mooncussers, setting false

Hull's Oregon House, *right*, began attracting visitors to Hull Village before there was a main thoroughfare stretching the length of the peninsula.

lights on shore and murdering their prey in order to steal the riches on board their vessels. (If the moon was too bright it shed light on the evil intentions of these shore-based pirates, earning them their nickname. On nights like that, they cussed at the moon.) The town's lifesaving heritage, of course, destroys all such notions; centuries from now, historians will still be praising Joshua James and the men of Hull as some of the greatest of America's lifesavers.

Fiercely independent, the people of Hull found a unique answer to the pre-Revolutionary War call to boycott and destroy all British tea, as they "made it clear that their quarrel was with the duty, not the tea," writes Benjamin Woods Labaree in *The Boston Tea Party*. They kept the tea, as supplies were hard to come by at the "end of the earth," and decided at a town meeting that once the British duty on the tea was repealed, they would "in equal terms, in (tea) as in all other articles, give the preference to England, whose true interest we have always considered as our own."

In 1786, that independent spirit inspired the people of Hull to attempt to secede from the infantile United States and form their own sovereign nation.

As late as 1872, Hull Village remained almost an island unto itself, separated from the rest of the peninsula at Stony Beach at the highest of

The first passenger trains arrived in Hull in 1880, solidifying the connection among the otherwise independent small settlements along the peninsula.

tides. That year, after the wreck of the bark *Kadosh* on Harding's Ledge, burial agent Lewis P. Loring opted to carry the bodies of the sailors who had perished as a result of the wreck to Hingham for interment, rather than risk having his wheels sink into the wet sand of the Stony Beach isthmus and be lost with the incoming tide.

Along the way, he passed the young settlements in the alphabet streets, a grid laid out in the 1840s as an intended seasonal resort. It would take nearly a century to fully develop, as Americans had yet to accept vacationing for its own sake as an acceptable part of life. The developers, to simplify matters, labeled the streets with the letters of the alphabet rather than thinking up names for them all. Only one street shows an alternate name on turn of the century Sanborn fire insurance maps. T Street is listed as "T, or Triton" street.

A second fishing station had by now grown up around Green and Atlantic Hills, and slowly the two ends of the peninsula would be brought together culturally.

Thanks to the laying out of Nantasket Avenue in 1870, people from Hull Village could more easily connect with their counterparts in places like West's Corner, named for shopkeeper Charles West, where a tidal mill had been in operation from 1679.

With hotels like the Rockland House and the Atlantic House attracting visitors to the southern end of the beach, and the Nantascot House, Oregon House and the Mansion House at Pemberton luring them to the other extremity, it did not take long for railroad and steamship companies to focus in on the potential for their businesses in Hull. The town's first passenger railroad in 1880 connected the steamboat wharf at Nantasket to the southern base of Allerton Hill, where yet another secluded seasonal community had begun to grow. Later that year, another company attempted to run a line from Allerton Hill along Spring Street and through Hull Village; the proudly defiant citizens there, though, forced the train to take an alternate route, around the exposed northeast base of Souther's Hill, to reach Pemberton. For fifty-seven years, winter storms playfully tossed six- and seven-ton boulders onto the tracks, mocking the railroad executives.

The coming of the train provided the first true link between the small settlements along its line, shortening transportation from end to end by hours. Most of the stops on the run of the South Shore, then Old Colony, and then New York, New Haven and Hartford line were merely descriptive terms: Surfside, Whitehead, Waveland, Bayside and Stony Beach. Others, Pemberton and Allerton, were named for early visitors to the harbor, while one, Kenberma, was named for the three children of an early land developer, Kenneth, Bertha and Mary.

Up until the time of World War II, life in Hull remained exceedingly local in nature. Some settlements, like Hobartsville along the bay between A and Q Streets, melded into others, while others, like West's Corner, named for shop owner Charles E. West's store (now an antique shop) and not for any geographic distinction, remained culturally isolated. The town's newspapermen collected contributions from residents in each section of town and printed them as social columns under the headings of Hull Village, Green Hill, Kenberma, Nantasket and so forth.

When the war hit, the town saw a boom in construction that filled in the gaps between the tiny communities. Defense workers building ships in local yards needed homes close by, and Hull had land to spare. Rows of similar houses up and down Manomet and Samoset Avenues stand out as examples. It took a global war, but finally, Hull had become a complete community.

Although the settlements have now grown together, and boundary distinctions are not as clear as they once were, the townsfolk in Hull still hold the names and identities of their neighborhoods close to their hearts. Improvement societies, large and small, active and not so active, boast of their territory's natural beauty, from Rockaway to Green Hill to Allerton to Pemberton. The Hull Historical Society has in its collection the handwritten records of the Pemberton organization's notes dating all the way back to the 1950s.

Civic improvement projects take place all throughout the town all year long, as evidenced by the new signs at the base of Allerton Hill and the entrance to Hull Village and cleanups at Straits Pond and the Village Park, among others. Although unified for the greater good of the town of Hull, residents here have yet to let go of their neighborhood pride, and well they shouldn't.

Back between the hills, where the Hull settlement began, the people of the Village stand out as the staunchest defenders of their terrain. Whenever a new face comes to live on Spring or Main, they must meet with the townies to learn the responsibilities of citizenship they take on by becoming a member of that community. Even then, the villagers joke, it will be a while before a new resident is given "the key."

In years past, folks talked of a gate at the entrance to the Village. People on the outside believed the gate was locked at night so that the people of the Village could not escape, especially when the moon was full; the people on the inside knew that they had locked it so that no one from the outside could get in.

What began as a three-man fishing station in 1622 has blossomed into a year-round settlement of more than ten thousand Hull citizens. Each summer, thousands of visitors walk our beaches, bicycle up our hills to admire our ocean views and frequent our restaurants and museums, but they will never see the inner beauty of Hull. They will never understand what it means to grow up and grow old in one of our many beautiful, historic, enchanting neighborhoods.

Diversity

To say that Hull has always been a place devoid of discrimination would be naïve, for after all, before Scituate's Chief Justice William Cushing convinced the Commonwealth of Massachusetts to abolish the practice in 1790, those Hull residents who could afford to owned slaves.

In most cases, Hull folk have followed the general trends of the country in regard to the treatment of women and minorities. On August 27, 1898, the *Hull Beacon* reported that, "A colored gentleman was refused admission to the policeman's ball last Tuesday night at Nantasket, and upon manifesting his indignation at race discrimination he was ejected."

Although Hullonians have followed those general trends since the time of the community's settlement, when we look to the town's past we should be proud of certain moments and events that shocked the sensibilities of even the most learned and open-minded people of the time.

Although it may seem trivial today, in 1881 the Hull Yacht Club admitted the first African American in any such East Coast organization. George G. Garraway, the owner of the twenty-foot catboat *Charlotte*, was a popular member of the club. Just a little more than a half century ago African Americans were still segregated from the rest of the population in schools across the country, could not play Major League baseball and fought in all-black units in World War II. To think that the members of the Hull Yacht Club in 1881 were able to see past the color of Garraway's skin and ask him to join them is simply amazing.

A smaller organization, the Hull Mosquito Yacht Club, advertised itself as the first such organization in the world to admit women to membership.

Massachusetts Yacht Club, Hull, Mass.

The Hull Yacht Club was the first club to admit an African American person to membership in the United States, if not the world.

Its rolls in 1898 included at least one woman, a Mrs. Nash. The move may have been simply a marketing ploy by the smaller organization in an attempt to undercut the powerful Hull Yacht Club, but the idea of admitting female membership in a traditionally male-only organization broke new ground.

Perhaps the lonely solitude of life on the Hull peninsula led to a greater understanding of cultures and religions, for it took a hardy type to brave a Nantasket winter two hundred years ago. Was the fishing that good? Were cod and haddock so plentiful that our ancestors felt compelled to stay in what the people of Hingham referred to as the "Moon village at the end of the earth" rather than move to larger, more established fishing centers like Gloucester or Provincetown?

Hull folk tolerated each other because they had nowhere else to turn in times of need. When storms hit, the Atlantic Ocean claimed Stony Beach as temporary sea floor, leaving no land escape route from the Village. Fleeing by boat during a nor'easter was, of course, impossible. All people could do was huddle together in their houses nestled between the hills, relying upon each other for food and supplies until the sun broke through the clouds. That toleration led to respect, and respect led to friendship and camaraderie.

By the late 1800s, Hull had become incredibly diverse for its size. Two men living in Hull had charged up the Italian peninsula with Garibaldi in that country's fight for freedom from oppression. One Austrian man had jumped ship from the French navy, only to wash up on Hull's shore and become the progenitor of the Mitchells, what is today still one of the town's most recognizable and respected names. Several Irish immigrants fleeing the famines of the late 1840s settled in town. The James family descended from William Jaames—with two "a"s—who came directly from Holland.

The above list may not seem to us today as being very diverse since they were all of white European stock, but would the Mitchell family have become what they are today in Hull had John Mitchell settled in Brahmin Boston instead of taking up wrecking off Nantasket Beach?

Hull's resident poet, John Boyle O'Reilly, spoke of the town's diversity on December 22, 1888, at a dinner given by the Hull Yacht Club at the Parker House in Boston, in honor of Captain Joshua James and the rest of the Hull volunteer lifesavers. The membership had assembled to thank and congratulate the lifesavers for their efforts during the Great Storm of November 25–26, 1888, when they rescued twenty-eight sailors from six ships in thirty-six continuous hours of searching, rowing and rescuing.

The brave men who dared face all this hardship were Captain Joshua James, Eben T. Pope, Osceola James, George Pope, Eugene Mitchell, Eugene Mitchell Jr., George Augustus, Alonzo L. and John L. Mitchell, Alfred and Joseph and Louis Galiano, Frank James, and William B. Mitchell. The eloquent orator who preceded me seemed to exclude all but Anglo-Saxons from sympathy with this bravery. I do not care whether a man is an Anglo-Saxon or not, if he be a hero. Carlyle says that a hero makes all but petty men forget the bonds of race and class. From the hero all small limitations fall away. His note meets a response in every man's heart…

And as to Anglo-Saxons, let me speak for the men of Hull—the men who pulled the oars in Captain James's boat—for I have the honor to know every one of them as an old friend. I know that the Jameses are Dutchmen by blood; that the Mitchells are Austrians; that the Popes are Yankees, that the Augustuses are from Rome, and the Galianos also are Italians. But what of their blood and their race? These brave men are neither Dutch nor Irish—they are Americans. And the men of Hull are types not only of Massachusetts, but of America. A section of Hull is a section of the nation.

The "Moon village at the end of the earth" may have provided for some laughs for people not living between the shielding hills of Hull Village in the past, but that settlement allowed for people of many, if not all, types to try to make their way in the United States, while other sections of the country fought off diversification. Hull may not have been the most cosmopolitan community of all, but its isolation and the tolerant nature of its inhabitants caused it to be more diverse than many neighboring communities.

Wrecker, Lifesaver, Hero

The sands of time can be cruel to the heroes of local history. The grains can bury the names and accomplishments of people who dedicated their lives to the improvement of small towns, who thought not only of themselves but also of the future and the people who would come after them. In a town like Hull we may come across their names while glancing at town records or passing by the town cemetery, but for the most part, we have forgotten many. Such has been the case with one of Hull's most influential and powerful personalities, Captain Moses Binney Tower.

Moses Tower was born in Hingham on April 26, 1814, the second child of Moses and Mary Binney Tower. Moses the younger spent his childhood at the family home on Hobart Street on Great Hill, where his father kept a farm. When he was just eleven years old, he lost his mother, who died two days short of what would have been her thirty-fifth birthday. Six months later, on Christmas Day 1825, his father remarried, exchanging vows with Abigail Andrews Gould of Hull.

Moses could not have been very happy at home. The family never did have much money, but nevertheless had grown to number six children by 1828. Moses, now fourteen, did not want to spend the rest of his life tied to the soil, so he left home to commune with his first real love, the sea. It was a relationship that would last for the next seventy years.

He joined the crew of a mackerel-fishing schooner in Hingham Harbor, starting out as a cook. As the years went by, he learned all he could about the business, becoming captain and finally owner of his own

Hull's telegraph station atop Telegraph Hill predated Samuel Morse's code system, using a series of paddles bent in varying directions to relay messages into the harbor. When the time came to lay a telegraph cable to the city, Moses Tower was the man who did it.

ship. His penniless childhood had served him well; he understood the value of money at an early age and the virtues of saving it as well.

He also excelled at making money. On June 10, 1838, Moses married Olive Gould Cushing of Hull. The next year he spent $800 on the purchase of the venerable Gould house on the corner of Mount Pleasant and Main Streets, a large two-story dwelling that had been standing since 1675. He began to expand the house immediately and converted it into one of Hull's first hotels, the Nantascot House. The

Hull's cemetery, shown here in 1938, was once known as one of the most beautiful on the South Shore, thanks to the elm trees planted there by Moses Tower.

innkeeper specialized in letting boats to amateur fishermen. Every summer brought hundreds of people from Boston, many hoping to tie into a mackerel or two.

But Moses did much more in Hull than simply run a hotel. Before there was a Hull Garden Club he became a one-man beautification committee, planting American elm trees in the town cemetery and outside of his hotel, one of which is still standing on what is now an empty lot next to the Hull Public Library. In later years the cemetery became widely known on the South Shore for its aesthetic beauty. Unfortunately for current Hull residents, most of the country's American elms were destroyed by Dutch elm disease, caused by a fungus accidentally introduced and then spread from tree to tree by native elm bark beetles about the year 1930.

Moses also helped to modernize the town, laying one of the first telegraph lines in the country from the aptly named Telegraph Hill to

Those elm trees were eventually wiped out by Dutch elm disease, but not before this particular Veterans Day observance shortly after World War I.

the Chamber of Commerce in Boston. He also served Hull as the town coroner, assessor, school committee member and selectman, as well as handling the job of commissioner of wrecks for Plymouth County.

As town representative to the state in the 1840s, he helped to create a Hull legend. Hull in those days usually enrolled less than fifty voters, and most of them worked as lighters and fishermen, sometimes spending days at a time on the sea. One gubernatorial election came down to a deadlock, with only Hull not reporting in. The town's fishermen came in to shore, visited the polls, and Representative Tower cast the deciding vote for Marcus Morton as governor of Massachusetts. From then on, the town became known as the political barometer for every election, and proudly lived by the motto, "As Hull goes, so goes the state."

Perhaps some of Tower's greatest accomplishments, though, came in connection with the Humane Society of the Commonwealth of Massachusetts. By the early 1840s, Moses had been chosen as the first keeper of the society's lifeboats in Hull. It was at his urging that the society placed a boathouse at Point Allerton, an especially treacherous spot along Nantasket's coast. He took part in a number of heroic rescues, most notably that of the brig *Tremont* in October of 1844, alongside his brother John Wesley Tower, who had moved to Hull, William James (Joshua James's brother) and five other men who joined the lifesavers en route to the damned vessel. As the leader of the crew, Moses received ten dollars and a gold medal, simply one of many. He also often opened his hotels to shipwrecked sailors, feeding them, clothing them and sending them on their way.

During these years the captain formed a lifelong friendship with young Joshua James (who, coincidentally, lost his mother at about the same age Tower had lost his), who would become Hull's most famous lifesaver. Although Tower would leave town in 1856, their bond would remain for almost another half century. The *Hull Beacon* reported on April 23, 1898, "Captain Moses B. Tower has presented Captain Joshua James, of the lifesaving station, a beautifully ornamented swordfish-sword, which is about twenty-eight inches in length." It was a gift of the sea, from one of her own to another.

In November of 1856, Moses and his family moved to East Boston, purchasing the Samuel Hall house. He continued in the fishing industry, owning a fleet of ships (the *William Daisley*, *Olive G. Tower* and *Mary B. Tower*) that hauled in mackerel in the summer and sailed to Jamaica in the wintertime to take part in the banana trade. He also worked as a submarine contractor and wreckmaster of Boston Harbor, excelling at both floating ships that had been stranded and raising from the depths anything that may have been salvageable from the harbor's many shipping disasters.

While in Boston, he also spent time as the director of that city's branch of the Pacific National Bank and signed up as an active member of the Boston Marine Society, a body devoted to placing navigational aids for the safety of boats in the harbor.

In 1879, the family moved again, this time inland to Auburndale. Although it was here that he would spend the remaining years of his life, he never forgot Hull. He even joined the fledgling Hull Yacht Club in September of 1881. Seven years later he retired from active business.

Moses Binney Tower passed away ten years after retirement, on November 28, 1898, two days after the terrible Portland Gale. His death could not have come at a worse time for his Hull friends. Joshua James, caring for survivors, assessing damage and identifying bodies, could not get to Auburndale for the funeral, and so didn't get a chance to say goodbye. Moses's body was interred in Hingham, the town of his birth, with full Masonic honors.

In the August 14, 1903 edition of the *Hull Beacon*, Floretta Vining described Tower as "one of Hull's greatest and grandest men. He did more for this town than any 20 men have done since his day. Up to his last hour he was interested in Hull." Yet we have no Moses Tower Lane or Moses Tower Park. Even his hotel has disappeared after being deemed unsafe and torn down in the early 1970s. All we have left to remember him by is his American elm, which is itself a monument to survival.

Sometimes it is just amazing what you can find when you dig through the sands of time.

Connected End to End

When Alexander Vining moved his young family to Hull in 1857, just four years before the breakout of the Civil War, the town was just taking its first steps toward becoming one of the premier summer resorts on the New England coastline. Colonel Nehemiah Ripley had opened the Rockland House just three years earlier, inviting inland residents to experience the beauty of Nantasket Beach. The Sportsman, Paul Worrick's coach stop on the county road from Cohasset, had been open for more than thirty years, but catered to a different crowd. Writer Ralph Waldo Emerson spent two weeks there in the early 1840s, and Marshfield's Daniel Webster was known to stop by while on his way to hunt ducks on the plains of Nantasket. Vining stared down the length of the peninsula and saw miles of opportunity.

Born in South Scituate (now Norwell) on May 11, 1817, Vining came from solid New England roots. His father, Alexander Vining Sr., a high school principal in East Abington (now Rockland), married Polly Jacobs, who could trace her ancestral line back to Nicholas Jacob (no "s"), who arrived in Hingham in 1633. Alexander, the only child of the union, married Fannie Margaret Raymond, the daughter of a prominent South Scituate sea captain. They lived in South Scituate until moving to Hull in 1857 with their two daughters, Floretta and Cora.

Vining decided to try his hand at the hotel business, taking over as proprietor of the Nantasket House, the building that once stood on the empty lot next to the Hull Public Library, on the corner of Main Street and Mount Pleasant Street. The Nantasket House had been a project of

Alexander Vining did much to shape the future of Hull while he managed the Mansion House at Pemberton Point.

Captain Moses Binney Tower, one of the town's most active citizens. Tower had purchased the Gould house, as it was known, in 1839, for $800, and advertised it as a hotel. A year after Tower moved to East Boston in 1856, Vining tried to pick up where Tower had left off.

Three years later, in 1860, Vining and his family moved again, this time to Windmill Point, where he ran the Mansion House, a hotel that preceded the Pemberton Hotel and Pemberton Inn at the town's westernmost point. At about that time, he also entered the leather wholesale business in Boston, becoming one of the most respected merchants in that city. He followed this trade until two years before his death in 1885. While in Hull, Vining served the community as a selectman for many years. The 1897 *Biographical Review for Plymouth County* complimented him by saying, "It is generally understood that he kept the best summer hotel along the beach, and in commercial circles he reached an enviable standing as a high-minded and upright business man who fully merited the respect and esteem which was accorded him by his mercantile associates."

In 1868, Vining set out to complete his most important contribution to the town of Hull, a project that, had he been vain enough, could have ended up with his name on it. Instead, since he was sincerely out to help the

Nantasket Avenue looking South from U Street.

Before Alexander Vining came to town, folks hoping to reach the Hull peninsula by land had to bypass a large sand hole near Strawberry Hill.

people of Hull, we today have Nantasket Avenue, and not Vining Avenue. Although his wife had died three years previously, just a month after the end of the Civil War, he continued his good deeds for the town.

On April 28, 1868, the Plymouth County Commissioners, the selectmen of Hull and other interested parties met at the Mansion House to discuss a petition to lay out a proper roadway from the Rockland House at Nantasket to Stony Beach.

> *On the petition of Alexander Vining and others of Hull, and adjacent towns in said County of Plymouth, representing that there is no well-defined road access across Nantasket Plains in said Hull, that the various paths or tracks used as carriage roads over said Plains are rough, stony, and unsafe for travel, and that the public good and necessity require that a highway be laid out across said Plains from "Mill Lane" at the southeasterly end of Nantasket Beach to Point Allerton Hill, thence around said hill on the westerly side to "Stony Beach," thence across said Beach westerly to the Cemetery, or the "Lane" (so called) or the northerly side of said Beach near the foot of "Telegraph Hill" and praying that a highway be located over the route aforesaid.*

The county commissioners, in holding the meeting at the Mansion House, had to travel over the various cart paths the length of the peninsula, and therefore got firsthand knowledge of the hardships of which Vining and the other petitioners spoke. Hull in 1857, although experimenting with summer hotels, was just then recovering from the shock of the American Revolution. Several families that left Hull with the evacuation of the community during the war never returned. The population in the 1820s was no stronger than it had been in the 1770s. As late as 1890, the town boasted only 450 or so year round residents. Two settlements, in the Village and at the southern end of town, thrived, but the area between Atlantic Hill and Allerton Hill remained largely vacant.

The construction of the County Road, or the Main Avenue, the Hull Road or Nantasket Avenue, as it was variously called, would definitely help Vining personally, as it would aid travelers, who opted not to come to Hull by boat, in reaching his hotel. It would not carry them all the way out to Windmill Point, but it would get them across the barren Nantasket Plains.

After listening to all concerns and taking boundary lines into consideration, the county commissioners closed the meeting and called for a follow-up meeting to be held on the first Tuesday in January 1869. There they laid out what would become a major portion of Nantasket Avenue.

Without much to use for waypoints, they "commenced to locate a highway in said Hull, beginning at a red colored stone set in the ground on the southerly side of Stony Beach near the bridge, bearing 29'10" east from 'Bug Light' [i.e., the lighthouse that stood at the entrance to the Narrows, on the end of the Great Brewster Island spit] and north 89'38" east from the Observatory [i.e., the Telegraph station] on Gallops Hill." They laid out the road using "a stone monument," "Boston Outer Light" and "the Beacon on the northeast bar off Point Allerton," an unmanned light structure that later fell over in a storm, as their locators.

The commissioners ordered the road to be a consistent fifteen-foot width its entire length "except on property of Holbrook and Ripley, parsonage lands, Sally Jones, Loring and others on Point Allerton Hill, where said location is to extend to the fences as they now stand." They also called for any telegraph poles in the way of the proposed roadway to be moved before November 1, 1869. The way was to be "leveled and covered with clay or other material suitable for making a hard and durable highway, to the depth of six inches over a surface of fifteen feet in width," properly crowned in the center to aid with water runoff. They then gave the go-ahead for construction: "The inhabitants of the town of Hull are hereby ordered to cause said highway to be worked and made safe and convenient for the public travel and to the acceptance of the County Commissioners."

The town carried the construction out in four phases. First, to be completed by June 1, 1869, they laid out the portion from its eastern terminus in front of the Rockland House to the base of Sagamore Hill. Second, they completed the portion over what was known as the "Sand Hole," a natural depression north of Strawberry Hill, tasked to do so by November 1, 1869. Third, they connected the previously built portions from Sagamore Hill to the Sand Hole by November 1, 1870. Finally, they finished the run from the Sand Hole to Stony Beach by November 1, 1871.

Alexander Vining had little time to enjoy the benefits of the new County Road. His Mansion House burned down two months later, on January 12, 1872. Vining relocated to Quincy, where he spent the rest of his life. If not for his initiative, the establishments at Windmill Point might never have become the successes they did. The railroads would follow, in 1880, but Vining and the people of Hull had already blazed the trail from the beach to the point.

Thompson's Wall

What we take for granted today usually represented a lot of hard work on the part of our predecessors on this long stretch of sand we call home. Such is the notion of sense of place, through which the same building, landscape or other type of location can mean vastly different things to different people over time.

What comes to mind when we think of the short stretch of the southern end of Nantasket Avenue that swings around past the former Hall Estate? Do we immediately think of the new Avalon development? Or are some of us old enough to remember the 1950s debate over whether or not to locate the high school on that land? And do some of us simply know the area for its ancient (and partially rebuilt) stone wall?

What did the people who lived in Hull think of the area in the late 1900s? No doubt many of them immediately thought of department store giant R.H. Stearns and his neighbor James M. Thompson.

A bridge existed over the Weir River inlet at West's Corner prior to 1854. In fact, it had existed for so long that the roadway from it, the town's boundary with Hingham, to the beach had been so worn that the locals petitioned the Plymouth County Commissioners to have it upgraded that year. Signed by Samuel Loring and others, the petition stated "that the public highway in said town leading from the Bridge over the Weir River to Nantasket Beach is very narrow and circuitous—praying the same to be widened and straightened, or new located, or altered, as the public good may require."

On Thursday, March 9, 1854, the Plymouth County Commissioners (Eben Pickens, John Ford and Isaac Husey) met at the Union House in

James M. Thompson's public spiritedness paved the way for the development of future businesses like the Villa Napoli on Nantasket Avenue.

Hingham to hear the concerns of the local citizens in regard to the roadway. Convinced "after viewing the premises and hearing all persons and corporations who wished to be heard thereon, it was adjudicated and determined that common convenience and necessity, and the public good, required said road to be altered."

The plans for the road included its widening by taking some of the land of several citizens and businesses on the eastern side of the existing roadway, measured in rods and links. The commissioners ordered the residents to remove all "trees, walls, etc." from the proposed new roadway by March 21, and ordered the Town of Hull to build the road by July 4. As compensation for lost land, they paid Francis Boyd four dollars; Patrick Arkley nine dollars; Paul B. Worrick, the proprietor of the Worrick Inn, ten dollars and seventy-five cents; E.S. Tobey twenty dollars; and David Cushing ten dollars from the county treasury. They also forwarded fifty dollars to the town to finance the construction of the road.

A little less than two decades later, on February 19, 1872, selectmen John Reed, Francis McKann and Edward G. Knight, at the petitioned request of Lewis P. Loring and others, announced plans to widen the part of Nantasket Avenue that ran from the "easterly end of the division walls" between the property of R.H. Stearns and that of his neighbor James Thompson to the terminus of the county road upgraded in 1854. (Stearns's property later become the Villa Napoli Hotel, and even later McPeak's Shore Garden, from which we today get Shore Garden Road; Thompson owned much of what later became known as the Hall Estate, named for General George F. Hall, a late nineteenth-century resident.)

Usually, if a property owner's land was to be altered, he or she could request remuneration for damages, a fair assessed value of the land lost. Thompson, though, decided to forego that pursuit, and ask the town for a special favor instead. "Said James M. Thompson," reads the entry in the town's roadway book, "releases claims for damages for his land taken to widen said highway in consideration of land in his front to be enclosed by him, and the right to remove such rock as he may want in building a wall upon said line of road." The town of Hull gave him four months to remove the wall already standing in the path of the proposed road widening. On March 4, 1872, town meeting voted to accept the changes described above, and James Thompson built his wall.

The Plymouth County Commissioners improved their road once again in April 1908, mostly so that Selectman John Smith could have a solid highway leading to his Nantasket Ice Company office, and a week later the Board of Land and Harbor Commissioners rubber stamped the Town of Hingham's request for a license to rebuild and widen the bridge over the inlet to Straits Pond.

Between 1854 and 1908, much had changed in regards to traffic flowing into Hull from the outside world. There was no coincidence as to why the former year saw a request for better roads leading to Hull, especially that section, for that year Colonel Nehemiah Ripley opened what would eventually be the largest hotel in the United States, the Rockland House, at the southern end of the beach. But in 1872, when the town decided to widen the access road to Nantasket Beach, the idea of Hull as a vacation spot was more or less still in its infancy. By 1908, the beach was in its heyday as a summer resort.

Were it not for men like Stearns and Thompson, willing to give up even small parcels of their land for the common good and growth of the community, would Hull have ever achieved its fame? Whatever notions it evokes today, James Thompson's wall at the southern end of Nantasket Avenue was once recognizable to the people of Hull as the wall that did *not* stand in the way of Hull's progress.

The Champ Leaves
His Mark on Hull

The one-two combination of his flamboyant, bombastic approach to life and his power-packed clenched fists turned him into America's first larger-than-life sporting hero in the 1880s. He never strapped on a pair of skates, caught a touchdown pass, nor slam-dunked a basketball, although his ability to hit a baseball did bring scouts from the Cincinnati Redlegs to the streets of Boston, the streets of his youth, for a look-see. He won his fame instead as a practitioner of the basest form of sport, as a bare knuckles prizefighter.

He stood defiantly incongruous in a time reputedly known for its class and elegance, its refined taste and ethics. Donald Barr Chidsey devoted his book, *John the Great*, to this hero.

> *He was a drunkard, this god. He was a loudmouthed, vulgar, oversized bully. At least for the greater part of his life he was a spoiled, irresponsible, disagreeable roughneck. "A son of a bitch of the first water," one correspondent says, adding bitterly, "if he ever drank any"…*
>
> *In the days when nice little boys wore long curls and velvet blouses and lace collars and cuffs and posed for their portraits with their hands on the heads of faithful Newfoundland dogs, Sir Galahad was not the hero of the youth of America, in spite of Victorian efforts to make this come to pass. The hero of this age and the man who had the most influence on boyhood's wish fulfillment was John L. Sullivan, the Champion of the World.*

John L. Sullivan's lifestyle fit Nantasket Beach's rough and tumble establishments like a hand in a glove. *Courtesy of Dyer Memorial Library, Abington, Massachusetts.*

Hull was a happening place in the days of America's first sports hero, John L. Sullivan.

Born near Boston College on October 15, 1858, Sullivan grew to bear a striking physical resemblance to his mother, a gentle 5' 9', 180-pound giantess. (His father measured 5' 3", 130 pounds.) As a boy, he "spun tops, cheated at marbles, and had many fracases with other boys," writes R.F. Dibble in *John L. Sullivan*. Although his parents hoped he would study for the priesthood, he chose instead to learn the plumber's trade upon graduation from grammar school at sixteen, prospering until he beat up a co-worker after an argument. From there he picked up tinsmithing.

In 1877, at nineteen years old, Sullivan accepted a casual invitation from a friend to step into a prizefighting ring at a Boston theatre. With one punch he knocked his opponent into the orchestra pit, realizing then and there, as he accepted the cheers of the crowd, what his true calling in life would be.

He struck up what would be an on-again, off-again friendship with wrestling star William Muldoon, who promised to train the young fighter. Sullivan starred in Muldoon's variety show, offering $25 to any man who could last one round with him. By 1880, he had raised the stakes to any sum between $100 and $1,000. He offered the money to any man alive, but specifically challenged Paddy Ryan, the current American bare knuckles

Certain establishments along the beach were known to hire their wait staff for their fighting ability.

prizefighting champion. Ryan would make Sullivan wait two years for his title shot.

Because of the violent nature of bouts fought under the rules of the London prize ring, fight organizers had to search hard to find secluded locations to avoid the law, but needed spots accessible enough to attract gamblers to lay down their money. Sullivan fought on barges and in swamps, anywhere a screaming crowd of prizefight fanatics could both make as much noise as they wanted and hide from the authorities at the same time.

On February 7, 1882, Sullivan met Ryan for the title. Although originally set for New Orleans, Louisiana, officials barred the event from taking place within their borders the night before the fight, forcing the combatants, their seconds and one thousand fans to board a train for Mississippi City. The governor of Mississippi, learning of these plans, posted signs urging all good citizens to use shotguns, if necessary, to stop the fight. Dibble writes, "Fortunately, however, no good citizens were there, as the absence of firearms and the universal prevalence of betting proved."

Sullivan appeared in the ring first and presented his colors, a white handkerchief with a green border, with American flags in diagonal corners and Irish flags opposite them, surrounding an American eagle. Ryan made Sullivan wait in the ring for more than a quarter of an hour before he made his appearance.

Under the London prize ring rules, the contestants fought in a twenty-four-foot square bounded by ropes, watched by a referee and two umpires. Knockdowns determined rounds. After each round the fighters had thirty seconds to rest, plus eight more after that to return to the scratched line at the center of the ring (from which today we get the term "not up to scratch"). The referee disallowed head butting, gouging of the eyes, kicking or kneeing fallen opponents and hitting below the waist.

Sullivan made quick work of the champion. By the end of the third round, he simply began to push Ryan over; after the fifth, his seconds told him to ease up, for fear that he might kill Ryan. For that reason, he refrained from hitting him in the stomach. After nine rounds and a total of eleven minutes, Sullivan won the championship. As Dibble notes, Ryan commented that he had never been struck as hard by a human as he had by the young man from Boston. "When Sullivan struck me I thought that a telegraph pole had been shoved against me endways."

After the fight, the new champion leapt out of the ring and sprinted to his quarters to change into his street clothes, lest any official ever find out that he was the one who had beat up Ryan. Due to the illegal nature of prizefighting, Sullivan would spend the next few years talking his way out of courtrooms and jail cells.

For the next decade, though, he lived at the top of the prizefighting world. He drank excessively and married a showgirl, Annie Bates, in 1883. They separated quickly, yet did not divorce until 1908. He considered their marriage a draw. While still technically married, he carried on a relationship with a burlesque performer, Ann Livingston, who matched him drink for drink.

As he toured the country by train, beating up the local hero at each stop (where he would step into the ring and throw out his trademark challenge, "My name is John L. Sullivan, and I can lick any son of a bitch in the place!"), he gained both fame and fortune. His army of followers knew him by any of a plethora of nicknames and epithets, from "Sullivan the Wonder" and the "King of Fistiana" to the "Professor of Bicepital Forces" and the "Goliath of the Prize Ring." To meet a man on the street who had met the champ was just as good as meeting him in person; people proudly shook hands with men that had shaken hands with John L. Sullivan.

To his ultimate detriment, he became known as an easy man to touch for a few dollars, if he deemed the cause just. In an uncredited seven-page "History of the Catholic Church in Hull and on the South Shore," Father Robert I. Turner offers this story:

> One of the more remarkable ways used to raise money for the new edifice [of the proposed St. Mary's of the Assumption Church on Green Hill] was to secure the pugilistic prowess of the great John L. Sullivan who consented to a boxing bout for this purpose. Naturally, the great John L. won the match and went with a group of parishioners to present the purse to the gentle Archbishop Williams in Boston. The latter, however, was violently opposed to prizefighting and refused the money offered, else, perhaps, our church might well have been built sooner, and perhaps, might well have borne the name of one of the Heaven patrons of the famed pugilist: St. John or St. Lawrence.

Sullivan also impacted the life of another famous Hull summer resident, John Boyle O'Reilly. In 1890, shortly before his death, O'Reilly published his *Ethics of Boxing and Manly Sport*. A canoer, runner and fencer himself, he defended boxing "for its value as a developer of health and courage." He defended the publication of his book with the same reasons:

> So long as large numbers of our young people, of both sexes, are narrow-chested, thin-limbed, their muscles growing soft as their fat grows hard, timid in the face of danger, and ignorant of the great and varied exercises that are as needful to the strong body as letters to the informed mind, such books as this need no excuse for their publication.

O'Reilly viewed Sullivan, a fellow Irish Bostonian, as the ultimate fighter, a blend of powerful force and masterful boxing skill. "There never was, in the whole history of the art, a more remarkable or interesting boxer than Sullivan."

Sullivan's reign as the king of the prizefighting world came to an abrupt end a month before his thirty-fourth birthday, on September 7, 1892. The champion could no longer inspire himself to stay fit, in a time, according to Chidsey, one of his biographers, "of great corpulence, of gout, of sluggish livers, and soft muscles," when "men, drinking beer and eating huge piles of potatoes, were expected to achieve their second chins soon after their wisdom teeth…" On that date, a young California banker named "Gentleman" Jim Corbett dodged and parried his way to victory, never giving the older man a chance.

Sullivan, who had taken on all comers, specializing in fighting foreigners (including Charley Mitchell of England on the estate of Baron Rothschild in France in March of 1888), announced his retirement. "All I have to say is that I came to the ring once too often and if I had to get licked, I am glad it was by an American. I remain, yours truly, John L. Sullivan."

After losing his title, and his mistress, who saw that his best days had now passed him by, Sullivan indulged in his liquor like never before. William M. "Doc" Bergan documents in *Old Nantasket*:

> *One Sunday afternoon in July 1896, John L. Sullivan, who had lost his heavyweight crown to Jim Corbett, was having a drink at a table at Pogie's Saloon* [on Nantasket Beach]. *A stranger standing at the bar made an insulting remark to him. Sullivan jumped up from his chair. The man flew through the open door so fast that you could play pool on his coattails. As he was going out he grabbed the knob and slammed the door. John L. started an overhand swing right from the floor. His arm crashed through the door and broken pieces of wood and his fist hit the poor fellow in the back of the neck and knocked him cold on the veranda…A new door was put on the outside of the casing. The shattered door was tied back against the wall, permanently, and a brass plate affixed describing the incident in memory of John L. Sullivan and as a warning to others to keep out of the way of his overhand right punch…*

He toured on vaudeville for a while, and ran a saloon in New York which was visited but spared by Carrie A. Nation, an ax-wielding temperance advocate who sang songs as she smashed bars, tables and bottles. After the finalization of his divorce from Annie Bates in 1908, he married a childhood sweetheart, Kate Harkins.

A staunch Catholic, Harkins took Sullivan out of vaudeville and straightened him out enough to send him off as a temperance lecturer, where he could proclaim victory in the toughest fight of his life, "licking John Barleycorn." They moved to a farm in West Abington, where Kate died in 1917 of cancer.

Sullivan spent the last year of his life on his farm with an old sparring partner, George Bush. He woke up every morning, swung his dumbbells a few times, then vigorously brushed his hair. According to Dibble, he then *spent the rest of his day in eating unbelievable quantities of food, in smoking, dozing and refreshing himself in many other ways, in the utmost confidence that his morning exertions would soon restore the trim sinewy body of thirty years ago. He seems, in fact, to have become an unconscious convert to the most original of Bostonian religions.*

By the time Sullivan died, terribly overweight, on February 2, 1918, of a weak heart, dropsy and cirrhosis of the liver, his total earnings over the course of his boxing and speaking life had reached $1.25 million; on that day, the only money found on his estate were a five and a ten dollar bill, tucked underneath his pillow. The "Boston Strong Boy" had lived life the way he wanted, and touched millions of lives around the country, including many here in Hull.

A Tormented Soul

The sudden death of John Boyle O'Reilly on August 10, 1890, shocked the town of Hull, stunned the city of Boston and saddened the Irish-American population. No better description of the poet's final hours exists than that found in his biography, *John Boyle O'Reilly: His Life, Poems and Speeches* by James Jeffrey Roche, published shortly after O'Reilly's passing.

> *He was met on the arrival of the boat at Hull by his youngest daughter, whom he accompanied to his cottage, romping and laughing with her in one of his cheeriest moods. He spent the afternoon and evening with his family, and late at night walked with his brother-in-law, Mr. John R. Murphy, over to the Hotel Pemberton, hoping that the exercise might bring on fatigue and the sleep which he so much needed...*
>
> *On leaving Mr. Murphy, he said, "Be sure and be over early in the morning, Jack, so that you can go with me and the children to Mass at Nantasket"...*
>
> *Mrs. O'Reilly, who had been an invalid for years, and the constant charge of her husband, had been confined to her room for the previous two days with a serious attack of illness, and was in the care of Dr. [William H.] Litchfield. A little before twelve o'clock she called her husband, who was reading and smoking in the family sitting room below, to ask him to get more medicine for her from Dr. Litchfield, as she felt very ill and feverish. Dr. Litchfield had already left her medicine which had benefited her, but it was all gone...*

John Boyle O'Reilly had barely lived in his new "cottage" for a year when he mysteriously passed away. It would take more than two decades for the town to rehab it for use as a public library. The cannon in the front yard came from the 1872 shipwreck *Kadosh*.

Mr. O'Reilly returned with the doctor, who prescribed for Mrs. O'Reilly. As the medicine had no effect, her husband thought one dose might have been insufficient, as he had accidentally spilled a portion of it. He therefore made a second visit to the doctor, who, on renewing the prescription, said, "Mr. O'Reilly, you should take something yourself," as he knew that the latter was also suffering from insomnia...

What occurred thereafter is not known to anybody, but all the circumstances point to the fact that O'Reilly, unable to go to sleep after administering the mixture to his wife, drank a quantity of some sleeping potion, of which there were several kinds in her medicine closet...

Mrs. O'Reilly woke up after a short sleep, fancying that she had heard some one call her. She noticed her husband's absence and perceived a light in the tower-room, adjoining her bedroom. Arising and entering the

Just before reaching the Pemberton Pier by steamboat a potential buyer of the John Boyle O'Reilly house changed her mind, after being told it was haunted.

room, she found her husband, sitting on a couch, reading and smoking. She spoke to him and insisted on his retiring. He answered her quite collectedly and said, "Yes Mamsie dear (a pet name of hers) I have taken some of your sleeping medicine. I feel tired now, and if you will let me lie down on that couch (where Mrs. O'Reilly had seated herself on entering the room) I will go to sleep right away"…

As he lay down, Mrs. O'Reilly noticed an unusually pallid look on his face, and a sudden strange drowsiness come over him. Never suspecting anything serious she spoke to him again, and tried to rouse him, but the only answer she received was an inarticulate, "Yes, my love! Yes, my love!"…

Becoming strangely alarmed she aroused her daughter Bessie and sent her hurriedly for Dr. Litchfield. It was then about four o'clock. The doctor worked for about an hour trying to revive him, but in vain. He died at ten minutes to five o'clock. Dr. Litchfield and a consulting physician, who had been summoned at the same time, recognized that death had been caused by accidental poisoning. The medicine which had been ordered for Mrs. O'Reilly evidently was not that taken by her husband, as it contained no chloral. The supposition is that he had taken some of her other sleeping medicine which did contain that drug, and that he was ignorant of the quantity during the latter which might be taken with safety. The bottles in the medicine closet were found disturbed. Part of the medicine which Dr. Litchfield had ordered for Mrs. O'Reilly was not put up by him, but was some which was already in the house. In prescribing its use, Dr. Litchfield said, "Use that medicine which you have, or which I saw at your house when I called yesterday"…

The fatal error doubtless occurred when Mr. O'Reilly went to the closet to get the medicine for his wife.

The question as to whether or not John Boyle O'Reilly mistakenly overdosed on his wife's sleeping potions or did so intentionally will remain a mystery forever, for as Mr. Roche notes, "What occurred…is not known to anybody."

Author Francis T. Russell, in his collection of stories on famous Boston personalities of the turn of the century entitled *The Knave of Boston*, theorized that O'Reilly's death was a suicide, a desperate final act by a man whose vision for a cosmopolitan world would never come to be.

O'Reilly was a man who represented the best of Ireland in America. That is his lasting significance. He and others like Patrick Collins, Dr. Joyce and Hugh O'Brien, the first Irish mayor of Boston, were men of culture and integrity who, like the Germans of 1848, had come to the United States as political exiles. With their abilities and their firmness of character they assumed the leadership of their fellow countrymen. Those semiliterate masses who had swarmed across the ocean were, however, driven by economic necessity and not by political idealism. They had been forced to leave a broken land to become the lowest level of the new-world proletariat. The Irish immigrants in the eastern seaboard cities lived and died like animals. Their somber fate played itself out obscurely, below the levels of literary understanding.

O'Reilly, who had escaped lifetime imprisonment in Australia and became a hero to his own people, watched as his fellow countrymen turned to the inherent corruption of the big city political machine, trading favors for votes, to rise from the depths of the slums of Boston.

So it was that the men of great Irish tradition, men like O'Brien and Collins and of whom O'Reilly was the honored leader, were followed by the venal little men, the Honey Fitzes, the Coakleys and their blackmailing rings, the "Bath-house John" McCoys, the Dowds and the O'Dwyers. Curley, who liked to quote O'Reilly, admitted disarmingly in his approved biography that there wasn't a Boston City Hall contract that didn't have something in it for him during his four terms as mayor. For men of the integrity of O'Reilly and Collins this was the ultimate disillusionment. In his later years Collins turned to drink. O'Reilly, out of some deep inner despair, killed himself at the age of forty-five.

John Boyle O'Reilly stood out as an anomaly in an age of institutionalized racism, sexism, xenophobia and almost any other form of discrimination that can be defined. As an independent thinker, he was able to see past all of these differences and discern one common thread in people of all races, color and religions: humanity. Yet, as he stood nearly alone in his tolerance and acceptance of the rest of the world's population as his brothers and sisters, and the frustration of living in an inescapably closed-minded society built inside of him, he began to show outward signs of depression.

In his article, "John Boyle O'Reilly, the Boston Pilot and Irish Assimilation, 1870-1899" in *Massachusetts in the Gilded Age*, Francis R. Walsh details those signs.

Although contemporaries referred to his open, cheerful, and robust nature, his letters suggest a man troubled over the course of a life. Occasional letters refer to a desire to "escape and let the busy world go past." In a letter to another friend arranging a canoe trip, he wrote, "Let us have a couple of weeks to ourselves forgetting all the meanness and worries of the outer world." One might dismiss all of this as simply the occasional complaints that are a natural part of any life. But coupled with the fact that O'Reilly's nights were made miserable with continuous bouts of insomnia, a condition often connected with depression, these complaints suggest a deeper problem. In a letter to a friend, he described his problems with vertigo and his fears of another attack: "I cannot sleep more than thirty minutes at a time," he confessed, "and if this continues, I shall either break down or have to give up altogether and go abroad."

Whatever the case, suicide or accidental overdose, John Boyle O'Reilly's body housed an unsettled soul during his last few years.

Following his death, his family stayed away from their summer cottage on Main Street in Hull Village. Professor Thomas Markoe and his wife stayed in the cottage for at least one year in the late 1890s before an unnamed "Observer" presented the following idea to the editor of the *Hull Beacon* on August 4, 1898: "Mr. Editor: would it not be an excellent plan for visitors and Hullonians to work together to secure the John Boyle O'Reilly estate and present it to Hull for a public library?"

The movement for a John Boyle O'Reilly Memorial Library came and went with the tides over the next few years, until the crucial moment when the family decided it was time to sell the house. All through the summer of 1900, a committee led by *Hull Beacon* editors Floretta Vining and David Porter Mathews gathered support and prepared for the auction, which was to take place on Saturday, June 16, 1900, at 3:00 p.m.

Strangely, not a single bid was placed on the house. The committee explained their actions by stating that they had voted not to move forward until after a sale, expecting to purchase the estate from the high bidder. Another woman, though, had a different encounter, as told by the *Hull Beacon* for June 22, 1900: "A lady who had made up her mind to bid on the John Boyle O'Reilly cottage at the auction last Saturday changed her mind because someone told her, while sailing down on the Nantasket boat, that the place was haunted."

And so a legend was born.

The town would finally secure the cottage in time to open it as our public library in 1913. For fifteen years the house sat empty, with its trees, shrubs, and gardens overgrowing. Photos from this time period, especially in wintertime, hold an eerie quality, as we peek through the gates onto the abandoned estate and the crawling limbs of the barren trees. The appearance alone would make one believe that the place was haunted.

Yet what of John Boyle O'Reilly? Is it mere coincidence that generations of librarians have closed the doors to the building at night, whispering the words, "Good night, John," just before leaving? Can a story told on a boat in 1900 have kept its credibility for a century? Or have there been other "experiences" that the current and retired Hull librarians could tell us about, experiences that would lend themselves to the possibility of a tortured soul still wandering from room to room?

The next time you're in the library and the rocking chair moves on its own, a book falls off a shelf, or a page in a book turns by itself (all things that have been reported to have happened), you can search for possible reasons as to why it happened, or you can just take the position that many of our librarians have taken over the years: "Oh, think nothing of it. It's probably just our John again."

Elegance Unparalleled

On any given summer day in any given year for over a century and a half, Hullonians could watch as majestic side-wheel paddle steamboats wound their way down from the city of Boston to the pleasant vacation destination of Nantasket Beach, carrying hundreds and sometimes up to two thousand visitors per trip. Passing by the picturesque Boston Harbor islands one by one, chatting with friends as the sun's rays and a slight ocean breeze promised a day of delight, the steamboat passengers rode in opulence, surrounded by beautiful murals, lush carpeting and finely carved wooden seating. A trip on a steamboat alone was worth leaving the house for.

First established in June of 1818, the Nantasket-to-Boston run ranked as one of the oldest routes in the country. From the single steamboat *Eagle* that year grew a fleet of vessels that eventually carried one hundred thousand people a day to Nantasket Beach, topping out in 1921 with a season turnstile total of more than two million passengers.

The steamboats had a touch of romance about them. Even their names evoked memories of days gone by: *Mayflower*, *Myles Standish*, *Betty Alden*, *Governor Andrew*, *General Lincoln* and *Mary Chilton*. The saloon of the *Rose Standish 2nd* housed the last paintings of marine artist S. Ward Stanton, who went down with the *Titanic*. When the Cape Cod Canal opened up to seagoing traffic on Wednesday, July 29, 1914, that same vessel, captained by Hull's Osceola James, led a parade of destroyers, yachts, steamboats and tugs through a piece of bunting strung across the canal, cutting the ceremonial ribbon. Even the newspaper boys who hawked their dailies at the wharves before departure were carefully selected by fate to provide unexpected

The steamer *Nantasket* and its various sibling vessels made travel from Boston to Hull and back a breeze and a joy.

drama. When seventeen-year-old Samuel Kneeland, a graduate of the Hull Village School, died in August of 1898 of a kidney problem, he was found to be a direct descendant of King James V of England. For everybody who stepped aboard a Boston-to-Hull steamboat, the trip represented the best that life had to offer.

Well, almost everybody.

One passenger in June of 1901 felt so disgusted about his trip to Hull that he felt compelled to write to the editors of the *Hull Beacon* for help.

> *To the Editor: After smoking on the forward deck of the General Lincoln today I approached the drinking tub for a draught. I always do this gingerly, as I do not fancy drinking from a common trough, but on this occasion I was repelled altogether. I had to wait for a big untidy deckhand who had evidently had a night out with resultant "hot coppers." He leaned over the tub and scooped up several cups full, drizzled and drooled and slobbered in the most disgusting fashion and wound up by throwing half a cup full back in the tub. That settled me and I went to the ladies' cabin and took a swallow of the flat, un-iced water that is provided there...The company ought to protect the health and make cleanliness*

Hingham, Hull & Downer Landing Steamboat Company.

BOSTON, JANUARY 1, 1883.

THE Annual Meeting of the Stockholders of the HINGHAM, HULL AND DOWNER LANDING STEAMBOAT COMPANY, will be held in the Committee Rooms of the Security Safe Deposit Company, Equitable Building, this City,

On WEDNESDAY, January 10th, 1883, at 11 o'clock, A. M.,

for the Election of Officers, and the transaction of any other business that may legally come before the meeting.

GEORGE P. CUSHING, Clerk.

Managing and running the Hull-to-Boston steamers was big business, as this postcard meeting notice would indicate.

and decency possible by abolishing those old tubs which are relics of the past and unsanitary days and substitute drinking tanks such as are on the Mayflower and also put a little ice in the tanks on warm days. [Signed] *Daily Tripper.*

From time to time, travelers could expect to find themselves stranded, or possibly even have a boiler blow their ship to bits. On July 11, 1871, the ferry *Westfield* exploded in New York Harbor, killing 104 passengers. On June 28, 1880, the *Seewanhaken* blew as well, killing 62. And when *General Slocum* decided it was time to go, he took 1,180 pleasure voyagers with him, including 400 children. Luckily, though, according to former Hull police chief Daniel Short's *Brief History of Early Steamboat Navigation*, the Hull steamboats "established a safety record second to none having never lost a life in over one hundred years of operation."

Well, almost never.

In July of 1901, Brother Louis Kirchner of the sacristan mission church in Roxbury stood on the deck of the *Myles Standish* on his return trip to Boston after a particularly beautiful summer's day. As the steamer passed within 250 yards of Long Island, a rifle shot cracked through the air and a bullet lodged itself in the good Brother's chest, felling him immediately to the deck. U.S. Army soldiers practicing with their Krag-Jorgensen rifles at Fort

Nantasket's Steamboat Wharf greeted thousands of visitors daily for decades.

Strong had let one get away. Before the boat could get him to Massachusetts General Hospital, Brother Kirchner bled to death.

In fact, though, Hull's steamboats probably contributed more to the growth of the town as a summer resort than any other entity. They predated the trains by more than half a century, which began running on July 10, 1880, to supplement the steamboats, originally running from the Nantasket Steamboat Wharf to Allerton Hill and back. In September of that year, the tracks were extended to reach out to Pemberton Point and the steamboat wharf at that end of town. The train ran for almost a year between Nantasket and Pemberton before connecting with Hingham. They carried high numbers of passengers to town in a short amount of time, and as "Doc" Bergan states in *Old Nantasket*, "The Nantasket Beach Steamboat Company was the finest asset Nantasket ever had."

Hull's steamboat line almost came to a tragic end on Thursday, November 28, 1929. The Nantasket Beach Steamboat Company had placed their six boats alongside the Nantasket Steamboat Wharf for the winter season, shutting down service until the spring as usual. That Thanksgiving Day, most of the townsfolk had traveled to Scituate to watch the Hull Athletic Association's football squad take on the Scituate Townies. Unfortunately for the steamboat company, most of the town's firefighters were good football players.

To this day, mystery still clouds the start of the great conflagration that claimed five of the six boats. The steamboat company kept its personnel on

Stately and beautiful before the 1929 fire that destroyed the Hull steamer fleet, the *Rose Standish* was hardly identifiable after the blaze ended.

the payroll year-round, so on that day the ships' captains for the most part were on the wharf. Some were reading, others dozing, but none expected what was to come. Captain James McNamara of the *Nantasket* was the first to react, startled from his newspaper by the frenzied screaming of a gull. Looking up he spotted flames leaping out from a shed near the *Betty Alden*, and sounded the alarm to alert the other captains. They turned on the pier's fire hoses, but the pathetic trickle of water did not help. By the time one of them could reach the fire alarm box to alert the town firefighters, the *Betty Alden* had been engulfed.

Grabbing axes, the captains and mates hacked away at the mooring lines in an attempt to set the boats adrift from the wharf, but due to the low tide, the steamers were sitting firm in the mudflats. Within minutes, the *Nantasket*, *Mary Chilton*, *Old Colony* and *Rose Standish* had been swallowed by flame. Only the *Mayflower*, sitting upwind, could be pulled away by a tugboat to safety. A fireboat from Boston worked its way down the Weir River, but could not get close enough to help.

Soon the inferno spread to include nearby cottages, destroying homes as far away as Atlantic Hill and Valley Beach Road. Flying embers even hit the roof of St. Mary's church about a mile away. As news of the fire spread by radio, spectators jammed the roads to Nantasket so badly that firefighters from neighboring towns could not get their trucks through to help. By the next morning, the assessed damage to the town reached more than $2,000,000. But at least the *Mayflower* was safe from destruction by fire.

Well…

The *Mayflower* was grounded near the steamboat wharf shortly after the fire, and the land around it filled in. She served for half a century as a dining and dancing facility, a symbol of a bygone era. Somewhere during the early morning hours of Saturday, November 10, 1979, the old ship burst into flames and burned to the ground, taking with it the last vestige of that bygone era when steamboats ruled the waters around Hull.

Steamboats Ashore

As far as street names in Hull go, the Hampton Circle area of town holds relatively few secrets, yet causes complications that only the town's emergency response personnel and law enforcement officials can truly appreciate.

The five roadways that run roughly northeast to southwest across Hampton Hill have a straightforward nomenclature: they're all named for old Hull-to-Boston steamboats. In the days when the classy white highly-appointed steamers chugged their way from the city to the shore, they made their final approach to the Nantasket Steamboat Wharf by sliding gracefully between World's End Reservation, Rockaway Annex and Hampton Hill before pulling in view of the grand hotels and hurried activity that electrified the Nantasket Beach area. Although the Rockaway Annex area may have been sparsely settled at the turn of the century, landscape architect Frederick Law Olmstead had laid out the grounds for World's End on the Brewer Farm in 1893. Then just saplings, the trees that Olmstead planted now line the beautiful paths of the reservation.

And so it was that the people of Hampton Hill could sit on their waterfront porches and watch the steady parade of steamers bringing wave after wave of visitors to the shore, hopeful of finding some excitement either on the beach or in one of the many legal (or illegal) establishments on shore by the end of the day. The view at the end of the day must have been truly special, with the grandeur of the boats parting the water as they headed back to Boston with a summer sunset for a backdrop.

The *Governor Andrew* gave its name to Andrew Avenue; the steamer got its name from John Andrew, whose family owned extensive land in Hull.

Old Colony Road was named for the steamer of the same name, which was obviously named for the early Massachusetts political body. Lincoln Avenue memorializes the steamer *General Lincoln*, which was named for General Benjamin Lincoln of Hingham. Overweight, afflicted with a sleeping disorder that would cause him to fall asleep in the middle of giving orders to his troops and saddled with a limp after taking a musket ball to the ankle, Lincoln nevertheless played a major role in American history. As a favorite of General George Washington, Lincoln at different times oversaw the earthworks at Fort Independence in Hull, surrendered the entire southern half of the colonies to the British after the siege of Charleston, South Carolina (where he is still vilified), and accepted the sword of surrender from Britain's Lord Cornwallis at the war's end at Yorktown. Lincoln also later served as the Treasury Department's first collector of customs for Boston Harbor.

Mayflower Avenue derives its name from the steamboats of that name, and not from the vessel that carried the Pilgrims to America; the steamboat was named for that ship. As with the others, the name *Mayflower* was applied to several different vessels over the years, the final *Mayflower* being the only survivor of the Thanksgiving Day 1929 steamboat fire at the wharf. Grounded and stabilized, the "Showboat Mayflower" hosted dancers,

The *Rose Standish* was named for the wife of the military leader of the Plimoth settlement in the seventeenth century, Myles Standish. Standish set up a trading post in Hull in 1621, and as late as the 1890s, his descendants were summering in Hull.

singers, hypnotists and other acts for many decades before succumbing to its own early morning fire in 1979.

Standish Road calls to memory the belle of the fleet, the *Rose Standish*, named for the wife of the military leader of the Plymouth colony, Myles Standish. The last *Rose Standish* made history as the vessel that "cut the ribbon" on the Cape Cod Canal in 1914, captained by Osceola James, the son of lifesaver Joshua. Across the harbor at Hingham's Crow Point, a hotel bearing the same name anchored the high class resort and entertainment area known as Melville Gardens, named for Thomas Melville, an ancestor of author Herman Melville who had participated in, among other things, the Boston Tea Party.

Andrew Road memorializes the steamer *Governor Andrew*, named for John Albion Andrew, late governor of Massachusetts. Governor Andrew, born and educated in Maine, served as Massachusetts's twenty-third governor, elected by the largest popular majority ever received by any candidate up to that time. His term coincided with the Civil War, and through his guidance the state raised five infantry regiments upon the initial declaration of war, and many more throughout the war years. He may be best remembered for calling together the Fifty-fourth Regiment Massachusetts Volunteer Infantry, the first all-African American regiment to enter the conflict, under

The *Old Colony* evoked notions of the first settlers of Massachusetts.

the leadership of Colonel Robert Gould Shaw. The story of the Fifty-fourth has been most graphically retold through the movie *Glory*. Although asked to serve another term, Andrew acquiesced to pick up his law practice after the war ended. A resident of Hingham, he died in 1867.

While the crossing roads of Hampton Hill follow a logical pattern of naming, especially with the area's history with the steamboats, they can cause confusion when emergency calls ring out. Dispatchers must be careful to delineate between Andrew Road and Andrew Avenue on Hull Hill in the Village; until the end of World War I, Irwin Street, just east of Strawberry Hill, was known as Andrew Street. Should a call go out for Lincoln Avenue, the dispatcher must be careful not to confuse it with Lincoln Street or Lincoln Terrace at Kenberma.

If an emergency arises on Standish Road or Mayflower Avenue, care must be taken not to confuse them with Standish Avenue or Mayflower Road on Allerton Hill.

Got all that?

Pebbles on the Hill

What Riley Pebbles wanted, Riley Pebbles got, at least toward the latter half of his life. Things didn't start out so easily for him, though.

Born in Orford, New Hampshire, in 1823 to a poor family, Pebbles found himself lent out to a farmer in town at fourteen, to help support the rest of the Pebbles clan. He served the farmer for seven long but loyal years. According to the 1897 *Biographical Review of Middlesex County*, "Having been educated in the rough school of life, cramped and handicapped in his early days to such an extent as would have deterred most persons from undertaking any serious enterprise, he had to make special effort to overcome the obstacles in his path." Like many New England youths of the early-to-mid nineteenth century, Pebbles struck out on his own and became what Senator Henry Clay would have called a "self-made man."

Moving to Natick, Massachusetts, at twenty-eight years old, he learned the shoemaker's trade. At that time, the industry had begun its shift from the single backyard shoemaker in his "ten-footer" (a ten-by-ten shed) to crowded mass production factories full of machinery, noise and lowly paid workers. (By the 1920s, seven towns in the Brockton area alone would be manufacturing more than 25 percent of all the shoes being worn in America.) In 1853, Pebbles sunk $800 into his own shoe manufactory, taking the leap into the corporate world. His mechanical know-how—he designed and built many of his own machines—helped him to drive his business to astounding heights, selling more than 290,000 pairs of shoes a year, with annual sales averaging more than $500,000.

Men like Riley Pebbles lived the industrial revolution rags to riches story, starting out with nothing and earning their way to the top of the American economic pyramid. Some, like Pebbles, stepped on their share of toes on the way up.

According to the *Review*, "He gave employment to many men, kept ten traveling salesmen on the road for a number of years, and won a reputation the country over for making goods that would stand the test of time."

And, like many wealthy individuals of his time, Pebbles returned money and energy to the community in which he lived. He chaired Natick's sewerage committee for four years, served on the cemetery committee, was director of the Natick National Bank and helped incorporate the Five Cent Savings Bank. He freely gave money to his Congregational Church, designing and directing the construction of the church's edifice.

Yet Pebbles had a reputation in Natick, one that was less than flattering. The *Review*, an unorganized encyclopedia of prominent citizens in the county who paid to have their biographies entered, went well out of its way to defend the hard-hitting businessman.

That Mr. Pebbles does and should command the respect and esteem of his fellow-townsmen none can doubt. That he has enemies is also, perhaps, true. But what living man could take a leading part in the business, social, political, and religious affairs of his town for half a century without receiving some measure of censure? But even those who have most harshly criticized his actions are forced to admit that, whether in private business, where his success was almost phenomenal, in banking affairs, coping with shrewd investors, in church circles, with careful, critical brethren, or in matters of public concern, Riley Pebbles has almost invariably carried his point, forcing things to go his way twenty-four times out of every twenty-five. That he has made mistakes simply shows that he is human. But that he has tried to do right in the sight of God and man, even his most adverse critics must admit.

In sum, what Riley Pebbles wanted, Riley Pebbles got.

And so, when Riley Pebbles wanted a proper roadway running past his summer home in Hull, he let the selectmen of the town know it. He passed a petition around the southern portion of the town in 1897, and by the time he was done he had collected forty-five names, an amazing amount of signatures for a roadway petition in Hull at that time. Among the signers were Horace E. Sampson, a Civil War veteran; Mike Burns, the famous Indian fighter and proprietor of the Mike Burns Inn (also known as the Oakland House, on the corner of Nantasket Road and Nantasket Avenue); and David O. Wade, hotel man extraordinaire and known for putting on the best clambakes on the South Shore. After posting all the necessary notices, the selectmen, led by a young John Smith, met at Pebbles's home and walked the proposed roadway, taking down all the necessary information: whose land would be affected, where the turns would be and estimated damages to be paid out. On December 11, 1897, at a special town meeting, the citizens of Hull voted (if it could be described as such under the reign of Boss Smith) in favor of Riley Pebbles's request.

For those Hull residents who live today on Summit Avenue, Riley Pebbles is your patron saint. You've got today, what Riley Pebbles wanted more than a century ago.

The Father
of American Bicycling

Prior to the Civil War, the idea that a person could get away for a few days just for the sake of getting away simply did not exist. As a country of farmers, tied to the soil, Americans worked from sunrise until sunset, to get the most from their land. After the Civil War, the Industrial Revolution helped create a class of economically secure gentlemen and ladies, who not only found time to vacate their winter premises to relax and enjoy life a little bit, but also found no deviltry in letting their hands lay idle.

At first, vacationers traveled to where steamships and train lines could take them, places like Hull. Once at their destination they took it easy, soaking in the sun's rays, breathing in the ocean mist, and enjoying the overall atmosphere of life away from the factory or office.

Soon, though, visitors to spots like Hull realized that they could do more than just relax. They began to form societies and clubs, as people with common interests sought each other out to share their passions. Yachtsmen came together along the northeastern coast of the United States to form clubs, and when they discovered the game of golf, they formed sister organizations to the yacht clubs. Hull in the 1890s boasted whist clubs, fishing clubs, literary clubs and even the "Hardly Able Club," whose members figured that when the weather in the winter would keep them from outdoor activities, they were hardly able to do anything.

Yet, amidst all of the fervor and excitement and fancy living along the seashore in the Gay Nineties, one man stood above all others as the king of popular culture. His brainchild led to some of the most popular songs of the day, created heroes and took personal mobility and combined it

Albert Augustus Pope was a member of the prestigious Hull Yacht Club, which filled the local waters with beautiful sights each summer.

with the never before experienced feeling of unbridled speed, or at least that which had nothing to do with a horse.

His name was Colonel Albert Augustus Pope, and he brought the bicycle to America.

Born to Charles and Elizabeth (Bogman) Pope on May 20, 1843, Albert Pope could trace his American ancestry back to John Pope, who arrived at the Dorchester settlement in 1634. He dropped out of Brookline High School at fifteen years old to help with his father's struggling merchant and real estate operation. He then moved on to Quincy Street Market and later on to a shoe-finding store specializing in locating footwear for people with mismatched, oversized, undersized or otherwise unusual feet. At nineteen, he enlisted in the army to fight in the Civil War.

He had plenty of chances to "see the elephant," (experience combat) in the Virginia campaigns, with General Ambrose E. Burnside in Tennessee, General Ulysses S. Grant at Vicksburg and General William T. Sherman at Jackson, Mississippi. He was brevetted major for his valiant conduct at Fredericksburg, and then lieutenant colonel for his gallantry at the battles of Knoxville, Poplar Spring Church and before Petersburg, where he commanded "Fort Hell" and led his regiment in the last attack on that city.

After the war he returned home to Boston, where he began manufacturing and selling shoe manufacturing supplies. By 1876, he had amassed a small fortune.

The moment that changed his life came that very year. He decided to attend America's Centennial Exhibition in Philadelphia, a show designed to glorify the country's first one hundred years of progress. (Needing a patriotic symbol, the Exhibition's coordinators created the fictitious Betsy Ross, and made up the story of her sewing the first American flag.) Walking around the grounds, his eye fell across a penny-farthing, or high-wheeled bicycle of English design, and he immediately fell in love.

The following year he toured England's bicycle factories, and his mind was set. In 1878 he converted his Hartford shoe and small mechanical part factory to manufacture bicycles and began taking orders. The bicycle was not a new invention by any means in 1878. A Frenchman, de Sivrac, built the first bike in 1791, not much more than a board on wheels. Twenty-five years later German Baron von Drais invented steering. Sixty-one years after that, in 1879, H.J. Lawson designed the chain transmission. Pope's Columbia bicycles took off, beginning with a 70-pound, $313 model in 1878. He knew, though, that he would have to market his product to get it to really sell, so he opened riding schools and published the monthly *Wheelman* magazine beginning in 1882, devoted solely to bike riding, and edited by S.S. McClure.

He promoted bicycle excursions as healthy activity, though some doctors claimed differently, vilifying the "boneshakers" as the cause of bicycle hand, bicycle wrist, bicycle twitch, bicycle hump and dorsal curvature. Other physicians saw bike riding as a cure for any number of problems, from headaches and sleeplessness to rheumatism. The riders themselves even took up the cause. Polly Pettipoint, the founder of the Well's Ferry Touring Club, called the bicycle "a step toward the emancipation of women," as noted in John L. Loeper's *Away We Go! On Bicycles in 1898.* She urged every female to ride, because "cycling will build up your feeble frames. It will rid you of dull, unhappy thoughts." Pope knew as well, though, that bicyclists would need room to roam, outside of the indoor riding ovals that he and others built, so he underwrote most of the legal expenses for the litigation necessary to allow bikes on roads and in parks. He also fought for modernization of the roads themselves, building a stretch of macadam on Columbia Road in Boston.

He also understood that the product could not become stagnant, and worked hard to find ways to develop better machines. He developed stress tests to ascertain vibration effects on frames, the "stretchability" of chains and the friction tolerance of ball bearings. In 1892, he set up a metallurgical research facility to develop lighter and stronger alloys.

Although competitors had begun to ease their way into the marketplace (Irish veterinarian John B. Dunlop developed the world's first pneumatic tire in 1889), Colonel Pope stood on top of the bicycling world in the magical year of 1898, the year of the bicycle. At the height of the craze up to five thousand cyclists could be seen at Nantasket Beach on any given Sunday. Bicycling heroes consisted of the fast and the strong. A.A. Zimmerman set the speed record for the mile in 1891 at one minute and ten seconds. Marshall Taylor, an African American, set records for the quarter-mile, half-mile, one mile and two miles within the decade, but no one could keep up with Mile-a-Minute Murphy.

Endurance champions rode as far as they could as long as they could. Plugger Martin rode 1,466 miles in six days on an indoor track in 1891, and Margaret LeLong in 1896 rode her bicycle from Chicago to San Francisco.

Of course, the military saw potential in the bicycle. The U.S Army Signal Corps placed machine guns on the handlebars and created a mounted bicycle corps. The military wheelmen battle-tested their "glorious contraptions" in the Spanish-American War, but they failed miserably, stumbling across terrain horses handled with ease.

Knowing he had more money than he needed and figuring that the bicycle craze would go on indefinitely, the colonel invested in a number of philanthropic endeavors. He donated seventy-four acres of land and $1,000,000 to the city of Hartford for use as a park. He funded the construction of the Pope Dispensary at New England Hospital in honor of his two sisters, both of whom were physicians.

As an avid yachtsman and member of the Hull Yacht Club (he was distantly related to the Hull Popes), he put together a plan to cut a waterway from the ocean at Stoney Beach through to Straits Pond, and then put a drawbridge over that span. He envisioned using the pond as a protected harbor for Cohasset and Jerusalem Road yachtsmen. The plan never took shape.

In 1897, Colonel Pope suffered the loss of a seventeen-year-old son, Charles Linder Pope. In his memory he constructed the Pope Memorial Church on Jerusalem Road in North Cohasset, off of West's Corner, which still stands today.

Suddenly and inexplicably, the bicycle mania that had lasted for more than two decades slammed to a crashing halt in 1899. Although Pope had seen the future in the automobile, investing in and manufacturing electric phaetons and runabouts as early as 1896, his overextended bicycle business fell to pieces. He defaulted on his bonds, and his stocks were declared worthless. Reorganizing his finances, he entered into partnerships with A.G. Spaulding and John D. Rockefeller, but nothing could stop the death of the bicycle.

Pope lived until 1909, struggling to fight his way back on to the top of the financial world, but died on August 10 of that year in Cohasset, under monetary and emotional stress. His name has all but been forgotten, but in the late 1800s it was synonymous with shrewd business sense and ingenuity. He will forever be known as the father of American bicycling.

Four Centuries of Fish

If you have a secret you are holding onto, but absolutely have to tell someone or else you will burst, tell it to a fisherman. For fishermen are the greatest secret keepers in the world, especially when it comes to the best fishing locations. But try to tell it to a fisherman with a graying beard, one that has been around awhile, for the ability to keep that secret is what separates the novices from the legends.

The legends instinctively know where the fish are. Jeremiah Digges writes in *Cape Cod Pilot*:

> *A nose for fish is like second sight, or it's perhaps a synthesis of knowledge of weather, of the habits of fish, of some evanescent clue, come and gone too quickly for a man's brain to record it. Yet it's as real as two times two. Year after year a captain with a nose for fish will come in, his gunwales awash, when his less gifted competitors come in empty.*

In fact, fishermen have been known to hide entire continents in order to protect their secrets, as Mark Kurlansky recounts in *Cod*.

> *To the glee of the British press, a letter has recently been discovered. The letter had been sent to Christopher Columbus…while Columbus was taking bows for his discovery of America. The letter, from Bristol merchants, alleged that he knew perfectly well that they had been to America already. It is not known if Columbus ever replied. He didn't need to. Fishermen were keeping their secrets, while explorers were telling the world.*

The Basques, the mysterious, independent inhabitants of northwestern Spain, fooled the rest of Europe for centuries. They continually returned home with boatloads of cod, yet no one, not even the Bristol merchants, ever spotted a Basque fishing vessel at sea. In 1534, their secret spot was finally found out, according to Kurlansky.

> *Jacques Cartier arrived, was credited with "discovering" the mouth of the St. Lawrence, planted a cross on the Gaspe Peninsula, and claimed it all for France. He also noted the presence of 1,000 Basque fishing vessels. But the Basques, wanting to keep a good secret, had never claimed it for anyone.*

Less than ninety years later, in 1622, two "wandering Englishmen" by the names of Thomas and John Gray reached an agreement with the Wampanoag sachem Chickataubut to purchase the land that is now Hull. Not long afterwards, they baited their hooks and began to catch fish. Since that day nearly four centuries ago, not a calendar year has gone by in which fishing has not played a role in the life of the town.

From very early on, the fishermen of Hull became known for their mastery. According to Samuel Deane's 1831 *History of Scituate, Massachusetts*, the colonists at Plymouth sought the expert advice of Hull's mackerel fishermen, who taught them how to catch the fish by the moonlight off Cape Cod. Prior to seeking out the men of Hull, Plymouth fishermen caught mackerel so infrequently that they had chopped them up and used them for bait.

By the 1840s, three-quarters of Hull's population of 230 or so (compared to Hingham's 3,500) made their living from the sea. James Lloyd Homer, in his *Notes from the Sea-Shore*, quipped that amongst Hull's inhabitants could be found followers of almost any religion, including Sculpinianism, the worshipping of the dried head of a sculpin (a small, scaly and exceptionally ugly fish).

As the latter half of the nineteenth century wore on, more and more of Hull's master mariners began providing their ships and services to recreational fishermen. Samuel James, older brother of the lifesaver Joshua James, took groups out on his sloop *Crosby*, while Joshua Albertas James, the lifesaver's nephew, entertained parties on his steam launch *Gazelle*.

While out on his boat one summer, Samuel grimaced as he watched a perfectly good round file he had purchased fall overboard into the depths of the sea. To his surprise and delight, he found it lodged in the throat of the next fish he caught.

Hull fishermen have been keeping secrets since 1622, and the tradition continues today, with men like Cap'n Bob Dever. *Courtesy of author.*

Soon, fishing became the settler of disputes. In September 1900, sporting controversy raged in Hull. Members of the Hull golf and yacht clubs squared off in daily debates to decide which sport was king. They finally settled their argument by means of a contest. Basically, whoever caught the most fish won.

They set out at five o'clock in the morning and dropped anchors within twenty yards of each other off the Graves and fished for three and a half hours. Each type of edible fish earned a certain amount of points, while unpalatable creatures caused deductions. The largest cod brought an extra ten points.

When time was up, the contestants returned to shore to have their points tabulated by an impartial judge. Unfortunately for the yachtsmen, they had snared five sculpins, which cost them twenty-five points. Final score: golfers twenty-seven, yachtsmen fourteen. Golf officially became the king of Hull sports.

And then, of course, there are the fish tales. Perhaps it is the compounded stress of the exertion of willpower needed to keep secrets that make fishermen the great storytellers that they are. By embellishing a story, by talking about the "big one that got away," they are able to relieve some of the stress that builds up over the years.

Hull fishermen have always been known to tell such tales, as reported in the March 19, 1898 edition of the *Hull Beacon*.

Among the 38 cod fish caught by Messrs. Stephen Lowe and Captain Samuel James, was one weighing fully twenty pounds which the former gentleman designated as a serious fish...His friend, Mr. Simon Peter Lucihe, says that Mr. Lowe has been in serious mood ever since the consumption of the Morrhua vulgaris, and that its brain assimilating properties have prepared him to do the serious thinking of the nation. Who can tell what fish story the serious fish whispered in Mr. Lowe's ear? For many years Mr. Lowe was a diver, and it may be possible that the fish was an old submarine acquaintance.

And anytime a group of Hull fishermen got together, at least one good tale came in with the catch. According to the June 27, 1902 edition of the *Hull Beacon*:

The Hot Sun club of Nantasket went on their annual fishing trip last Monday with Captain Carroll Cleverly on his steam launch Gloria... While Mr. [George W.] Bates was down in the cabin, where he had gone, leaving his line in the water, Mr. [E.F.] Davis thought he would have some fun, so he pulled up the line and attaching a lager beer bottle, threw it in again. When Bates returned from the cabin he felt something on his hook, and commenced to pull it in, while the others waited expectantly intent on having the laugh on the fisherman, but when the hook came in view with an eight pound haddock attached the laugh was on them.

Sometimes the fish tales that appeared in the *Hull Beacon* have been bizarre, as is this one from the September 4, 1903 edition.

Captain Burchell of Nantasket, in the catboat Crusader, started out bright and early Tuesday morning with members of the Dogfish club aboard, bound for a fishing trip [off Nantucket]. While the boat was on the Rip off Great Point light, enjoying great luck with the fish, which seemed to be biting unusually fast, one of the members felt a mighty tug at his line. The boat was almost upset in the effort the whole party made to land the fish. In the midst of great excitement the struggling monster was landed in the middle of the boat...It proved to be the terrible red monster called the squeegee. It had the head and bill of a duck, the body and shape of a fish and wings and legs like a bird. It was supposed that this species of monster was long ago extinct. The scarcity of bluefish off Nantucket is attributed to its presence.

Other stories are simply unbelievable, no matter how many witnesses were produced. The July 24, 1897 edition of the *Hull Beacon* reports:

Wednesday evening at about eleven o'clock the sea serpent made his annual visitation to Nantasket Beach, at least so say a large number of persons who were attracted to the edge of the water by a black object about sixty feet from the beach. The monster appeared to be over fifty feet long and made a great commotion in the water. Over three hundred persons saw the animal and it is probably identical with the Marblehead serpent…

Another Hull fisherman has seen the sea serpent. The character of these gentlemen is above reproach and this is no fish story.

No matter what the level of fishing fanaticism, though, it seems everybody could enjoy a day on the waters off Hull. "Mr. Sam Silver expects a visit from Grover Cleveland soon. Grover desires to have a few casts for smelts," proclaimed the *Hull Beacon* on August 23, 1901.

For almost four hundred years now, Hull's one constant has been the fisherman. Kurlansky writes, "He is a captain, a navigator, an engineer, a cutter, a gutter…And he's a tourist attraction. People want to come to a town where there are men with cigars in their mouth and boots on their feet mending nets."

Today, although a much smaller percentage of Hull's residents work on the sea, the town still remains one of the best spots in Boston Harbor from which to fish, especially for the recreational or amateur angler.

Recently, while waiting to head out from the Nantasket Beach Saltwater Club to do some fishing with Cap'n Bob Dever of Elena D Charters, I was greeted by another fisherman down on the dock. "You're going out with Bobby? Good for you. He knows where to find 'em."

Yet all Hull fishermen, including Dever, must bow down to the legendary founder of the Saltwater Club, Ollie Olsen. I told Bob recently about an October 4, 1942 *Hull Times* article about the day Olsen had to come in early because his boat was dangerously overloaded with 608 smelt. His immediate question was, "Did the article say where he was fishing?"

"No."

"Damn! He's still keeping his secrets!"

If you can, find yourself a Hull fisherman when you visit the shore. Look into his face—the tanned skin, the smiling eyes and the happy, easy demeanor brought on by a life of freedom on the water—and know that it is the face of Hull, the heritage of our town's first four centuries. Let him regale you with his tales of churning seas and burned biceps from fish fighting. As he is speaking, realize that these stories have been told on this thin stretch of land for 375 years. And just like every other fisherman around the world, be sure he'll tell you about the "big one that got away," but he won't tell you where he found it.

H.D. Corey and His Wonderful Horseless Carriage

Hull summer resident H.D. Corey loved his Winton touring car. More than that, he simply enjoyed driving. In fact, by 1903, he and his wife had joined a new class of thrill seekers, folks of all ages who traveled the world on four wheels in hopes of meeting new people and seeing the things of which they had heretofore only read. They gathered together in touring groups for daily itineraries of exploration under the banner "automobile enthusiasts."

Of course, before the world could accommodate automobile enthusiasts, it needed automobiles. In 1805, Swiss scientist Isaac de Rivaz attached an internal combustion engine to a four-wheeled cart, coaxing it to move enough to barely crawl across a room.

Sixty-one years later Frenchman Jean-Jacques Etienne Lenoir raised the eyebrows of the world when he drove a powered carriage for six miles, although it took him three hours to do so.

In 1871, Dr. W.J. Carhart of Racine, Wisconsin, built a steam-powered vehicle that looked "suspiciously like the wedding of a buggy and a potbellied stove," according to Floyd Clymer in his *Treasury of Early American Automobiles, 1877-1925*. In 1877, patent lawyer George B. Selden introduced his first "horseless carriage," with its engine mounted under the front axle. By turning the steering wheel 180 degrees, the driver could move in the opposite direction. Selden quickly applied for a patent, claiming himself as the originator of the gasoline-powered car.

Charles and Frank Duryea designed and test-drove the first marketable automobile in America in 1893. That year they took their seven hundred-

In 1903, when Harold Corey led his lifesaving expedition across the roads of the South Shore, an automobile was an odd sight in Hull.

pound, four-horsepower, single-seated buggy for a ride through the streets of Springfield, Massachusetts, dodging pedestrians and horses by the use of a tiller. The original Duryea automobile can be seen today at the Smithsonian in Washington, D.C.

Scotsman Alexander Winton, the maker of Mr. Corey's car, settled in Cleveland in 1884 and began work at the Phoenix Iron Works. His engineering background, gained by toiling in the shipyards of the Clyde River as a young man and subsequently on ocean-going vessels, led him into the world of bicycle repair and, by 1891, bicycle design. By 1895, Winton had tested his first gasoline-powered bicycle.

In 1896, he progressed from two wheels to four, and in 1897 he formed and incorporated the Winton Motor Carriage Company. That year he engineered the world's first automobile publicity stunt, driving his two-

This gentleman, believed to be George Hobbs, had the carriage all set. All he had to do was figure out the horseless part.

cylinder motorcar eight hundred miles from Cleveland to New York in ten days. In 1898, he sold twenty-two cars at $1,000 each, the first American cars to be sold by a set production schedule.

The Winton cars sold well, although they did have their share of problems. Of the original twenty-two, number twelve would haunt Winton the longest.

Its purchaser, a young man from Warren, Ohio, exasperatedly listed the car's defects to the Scotsman after having it break down on him repeatedly on his way home from the factory. He stated he had finally, to his great embarrassment, settled for a team of horses to drag his vehicle to his front door.

By the 1910s, the car would be competing with steamboats and trains for transportation dollars, and would turn Hull's Golden Mile to an extended parking lot.

Winton, who never took criticism well, finally stopped the young man's rant by shouting, "All right, if you don't like the car, and you know so much, why don't you make a car of your own?!" as noted by Stephen W. Sears in *The American Heritage History of the Automobile in America*.

Nonplused, the young man, James Ward Packard, walked out of the office and did just that. His first car, completed on November 6, 1899, introduced to the world the reverse gear, marked as one of the great innovations in early car manufacturing. Long after Winton had been forgotten, Americans would still be purchasing Packards, trusting in the motto, "Ask the man who owns one."

Nevertheless, Winton continued to stand at the forefront of the automobile world, selling one hundred cars in 1899 and running a second publicity stunt from Cleveland to New York. This time, to assure his trip received proper coverage, he saved the car's second seat for reporter Charles Shanks of the *Cleveland Plain Dealer*, who sent daily dispatches back to his editor in Ohio.

Winton's sales soared, and the word "automobile" came into general use for the first time, thanks to Shanks's repeated references to the vehicle as such.

About this time, Winton's factory superintendent, Leo Melankowski, came to his boss to tell him about a highly talented young engineer looking for a job. The thin young Michiganite had already built his own car and, in Melankowski's eyes anyway, showed a lot of promise. Winton, though, had less regard for the young man and told him he had no room for him on his payroll. Rejected, but with his head held high as he thought out his next move, Henry Ford headed back to Detroit.

As the master of the marketing stunt, Winton knew early on that speed would sell cars, much as it had for bicycles. On Memorial Day 1897, he had thrilled the gathered throng at Cleveland's Glenville Track by blasting around the horseracing oval at the mind-bending speed of 33.64 miles per hour. In 1900, after he had earned the title of American racing champion by covering a mile in one minute, 14.50 seconds, he entered the first international automobile competition, the 354-mile Gordon-Bennett race from Paris to Lyons, France.

A lover of all sport, proprietor of the *New York Herald* James Gordon Bennett composed the race's twenty-four rules while in Paris to set up a French edition of his newspaper. Each country could enter up to three cars, with a minimum weight of four hundred kilograms, with the occupant weighing at least seventy kilograms.

Three Frenchmen, one Belgian and Winton entered. Only two of the five cars finished, both French, the leader coming in 90 minutes ahead of his countryman at an average speed of 38.6 miles per hour. The winner even had time to hit a dog, pull over to the side of the road, drag the dog aside, get back in his seat and continue toward the finish line.

On October 10, 1901, stilted engineer Henry Ford finally returned to exact a bit of revenge on Winton. That day in Detroit, the two raced one on one. Through five laps they remained side-by-side, one edging in front of the other. Then suddenly, during the sixth go-round, Winton's car overheated. Ford pulled away to victory, leapt out of his car and announced his retirement from racing.

Following that event, two of the country's most celebrated bicyclists, Tom Cooper and Barney Oldfield, raced on a tandem against the clock, surprisingly drawing yawns from the crowd. They could see that the bicycle's run had ended, as Daisy and her bicycle built for two had pulled over to the side of the road to make way for Lucille and her merry Oldsmobile.

Cooper retired, and Oldfield, a former bellhop, newsboy, elevator operator and boxer, looked to automobile racing for work.

His big break came in October 1902, when Ford asked him to drive his super fast, sleek "999" racer against Winton and three other competitors in a 10-mile contest at Grosse Point, Michigan. Taking one look at the 2,800-pound monster, which he would have to steer by handlebars, Oldfield said, "Well, this chariot may kill me, but they'll say afterward that I was going like hell when it took me over the bank. I may as well be dead as dead broke," quotes Richard Crabb in *Birth of a Giant: The Men and Incidents That Gave America the Motorcar.*

Oldfield won the race, establishing himself as the world's fastest human being, and Ford as a premier auto manufacturer. The following summer, Oldfield broke the one-minute mile on a dirt track in Indianapolis. For generations, traffic cops stopping speeding motorists would approach offending drivers and quip, "Who do you think you are, Barney Oldfield?"

Unable to keep themselves away from the excitement that an automobile would bring, Mr. and Mrs. Corey decided to purchase their Winton touring car. During the summer of 1902, they covered two thousand miles of European roads, and in June of 1903, they headed to Ireland to watch the fourth Gordon-Bennett race. (According to the rules, the country of the winning driver would host the next year's race. An Englishman won in 1902, but since England had already banned street racing, the event moved to Ireland.)

While in Ireland, the Coreys met with the Charles Jasper Glidden tour. Glidden, a New England telephone pioneer (who discovered, for instance, that women's voices generally carry better over phone lines than men's, and therefore women would better serve the telephoning public as operators) who that year intended to drive his car to the Arctic Circle.

The Coreys rode with the Glidden Company for 1,200 miles through England, Ireland and Wales before they returned home on business.

Glidden continued on to Denmark and Sweden, going as far north as Kommis, the southern edge of the Arctic Circle, as is documented in Glidden's article "To the Arctic Circle in a Motor Car," published in *New England Magazine* in January 1904.

On September 23, 1903, an eighty-year-old female resident of Hull (whose name in connection with this event has not come down to us) took a nasty fall and broke her hip. A nearby physician came quickly to her aid. He became frustrated, though, when he realized that, due to the frequent required stops of the electric railroad and the rocking and rolling of a steamship, a comfortable ride to a Boston hospital would be near impossible for the incapacitated octogenarian.

Mr. Corey, hearing of the doctor's plight, offered his Winton touring car for ambulance service. Together, they arranged the old lady comfortably in the tonneau, and set off for the city at 9:00 a.m.

American roads had not changed much since the first one had been laid out between Boston and Plymouth in 1639. "In 1903 more than ninety-three percent of the 2.3 million miles of roads in the U.S. were nothing better than plain dirt—horse-belly deep in mud in spring, thick with dust in the summer, frozen in iron-hard ruts in winter," writes Sears. Nevertheless, the stoic patient reported her ride in the Winton as more than comfortable, even enjoyable.

His good deed done for the day, Corey motored back to Hull to check over his vehicle and otherwise enjoy the early fall afternoon. No sooner had he entered the Allerton section, than a second doctor stepped into the street and frantically waved him down. He explained hurriedly that another woman in town had taken suddenly and dangerously ill with appendicitis, and that she must be operated on within two hours, lest her life be lost.

Corey took the doctor and the woman on board, reversed direction, and pushed the accelerator to the floor. Reaching top speeds of more than thirty miles per hour, they passed through the towns of Hingham and Weymouth and on into Quincy. When they reached Faxon Park, however, where they hoped to take some of the smoothest roads south of Boston, a policeman pulled them over.

Standing alongside the driver, he asked what the hurry was, no doubt making a quick reference to Barney Oldfield. In a scene that would play out hundreds of times for future generations of gazers at yet-to-be-invented television and motion pictures, the policeman cleared the way for them, escorting them to the Newton Cottage Hospital. The patient arrived in time for her operation, as the trio had amazingly covered twenty-eight miles in just over an hour.

Mr. Corey puttered back to Hull for the second time around 5:00 p.m., and watered down his tires so that they would not explode. Other than that one bit of attention, his car needed no maintenance.

In a town already known for its association with the saving of lives, H.D. Corey had found a new way to perform the miraculous, thanks to Alexander Winton, Barney Oldfield, Henry Ford and the rest of the world's automobile pioneers.

Old Home Week

It used to be in America that you could count on your children inheriting your farm and tilling the same soil that your father and grandfather had turned before you. You could assume that they would not stray beyond the borders of the town more than a few times in their lives. Who needed to? You could expect to see them marry respectable local young men and women from good, upstanding families and raise large families of their own, to continue working the same plots of land.

Then along came the Industrial Revolution.

Factories, constructed near ports and on rivers by entrepreneurs and "self-made men," needed workers. Immigrants, attracted by promises of instant wealth, flocked to America, the world's newest "land of opportunity," and fulfilled much of the factory owners' needs, but still spots remained open. The country was changing, growing more quickly than ever before, and that process required many, many pairs of hands to be at the center of the industrial whirlwind in the cities.

What little work could be found in Hull after the Civil War was seasonal. The hotels, amusements and other related vacation entertainment industries stayed active only as long as the temperature remained above fifty-five degrees. The lifesaving station stayed open all winter long, but employed only eight men. Spurred on by these conditions, advances in transportation that shrank time and space and subsequently made opportunities for adventure seem more accessible and attainable than ever before, and the lure of the new "big cities," generations of young people left their ancestral homes to forge new lives, rarely ever looking back.

Visitors arriving via the Pemberton steamboat wharf during Hull's Old Home Week celebration were greeted by this beautiful and symbolic arch.

In 1902, responding to the disillusioned lamenting of parents of such offspring gone astray, several Massachusetts towns adopted the idea of "Old Home Week." Governor F.W. Rollins of New Hampshire designed "Old Home Week," a mid-summer celebration, with the intention of bringing those children back to their roots, if only for a few days, to see that their homes were not places to hide from or of which to be ashamed, but, indeed, of which to be proud. In 1903, Hull, already boastful of its historical heritage, picked up the idea.

It had been two years since Leon F. Czolgosz had assassinated President William McKinley, a former summer visitor to Hull (he favored the Atlantic House), and popular Teddy Roosevelt now had a firm grip on the country's problems. In January of 1903, John D. Rockefeller donated $7,000,000 toward the search for a cure for tuberculosis. In February, President Roosevelt signed the law that created the Department of Commerce and Labor. In May, American public interest focused on the formation of Dr. Harvey Wiley's "poison squad," a special commission of the Department of Agriculture's Bureau of Chemistry charged with determining the effects of preservatives and coloring matter on food.

Old Home Week's organizers hoped to point out the historic high points, like the Old Town Hall, *center*, built in 1848.

On July 17, James McNeill Whistler died; three days later, Pope Leo XIII followed him to the grave.

In Hull, the new water tower at Fort Revere had just been completed, topped with a five-foot long weathervane in the shape of a cannon, designed by former lifesaver and current owner of Knight's Express livery service, James F. Dowd. In March, Floretta Vining, the self-proclaimed "Mayor of Hull," accepted an invitation from President and Mrs. Roosevelt to attend a "grand musicale" at the White House. By July, she would be entertaining the world's richest woman, Hettie Green, at Vining Villa on Stony Beach.

The executive committee of the Hull Old Home Week Association, led by President Otto J. Piehler and organizer David Porter Mathews, set out to make Hull's version of the celebration the most highly regarded in the state. They urged residents to notify their kin and to coax them back to their hometowns with promises of a grand series of events.

Throughout the town, wooden signs with painted numbers (that corresponded with a printed map) marked Hull's historic sites. Some of those sites, such as the John Boyle O'Reilly summer cottage, the old French fort on Telegraph Hill and the Massachusetts Humane Society boathouse which contained the surfboat *Nantasket*, can still be seen today. Others, like

The telegraph station atop the hill bearing its name stood in the shadow of the Fort Revere water tower, built in the same year as the first Old Home Week celebration in Hull, 1903.

the summer home of the Reverend S.F. Smith, author of the song "America," and the wharf at the East End of Hull Village, originally constructed in 1682, are somewhat more obscure.

All week long, beginning with Monday, July 27, the James Ladies' Orchestra performed concerts at the Town Hall, where visitors could also view a collection of relics pertinent to the town's history, some of which turned up during the preparations. "While excavating for the foundation of an arch of welcome at Hull Village, the workmen unearthed an old Indian tomahawk, made of stone, which was added to the collection of relics in the town hall," reported the *Hull Beacon* on July 31, 1903. The *Beacon* later reported on August 14 another accidental archaeological discovery of the same dig: "A cavity about 25 feet square, with solid clay walls, has been discovered where the old-home week arch of welcome in the village stood. It is thought to be the old cellar of the trading post established by Myles Standish in the early spring of 1622."

Both year-round and summer residents alike dressed their homes with bunting, flags, electric lights and Japanese lanterns, including the dwellings of the Galianos, Dowds, Mitchells, Cleverlys, Jameses, Lucihes and Knights. Businesses, such as the Oregon House, Cleveland House and Oakland

Families like the Galianos dressed their houses for Old Home Week.

House Hotels, Daley and Wanzer livery service and even the lifesaving station, all presented colors for the occasion.

On Sunday night, July 26, Lizzie A.R. Knight inaugurated the observance by reading a specially written poem at the Hull Methodist Church, but the true festivities began the next day.

A thousand spectators gathered at the Village Park Monday morning to hear the week's guest speakers, Governor Rollins of New Hampshire and John Davis Long of Hingham, former state representative, Massachusetts governor and secretary of the navy under McKinley during the Spanish-American War. Both failed to appear, sending letters of regret, read aloud by David Porter Mathews.

Mathews then announced the featured speakers who did show, including Lieutenant Governor Curtis Guild Jr., Representative Thomas H. Buttimer and Hull Town Counsel Joseph O. Burdett. Historian Fitz-Henry Smith Jr., who later would write *The Story of Boston Light* and *Storms and Shipwrecks in Boston Bay and the Record of the Life Savers of Hull*, spoke of the town's storied history, but focused mostly on Hull's claim to be the final resting spot of Thorwald the Viking, the tragic hero of

Even Hull's famous "wedding cake house" on Main Street brought out the colors for the occasion.

the Norse *Vinland Saga*, disputing Henry Cabot Lodge's similar claim for Nahant. (Professor John Moore, whose twenty-six chapter *History of Hull* had just completed its serialized run in the Vining newspapers, suggested that Thorwald had been laid to rest on Rainsford Island, pointing to the recent discovery of an entombed skeleton and sword hilt.) That evening, the association held an informal kick-off banquet.

On Tuesday, under delightful skies, Town Treasurer Clarence Vaughn Nickerson (who would remain a fixture in Hull politics for the next four decades as a member of the Old Ring) squared off his best nine baseball players against a team coached by Representative John Fitzgerald, a summer resident. Either due to Fitzgerald's superior baseball knowledge, or the younger Nickerson's political savvy, Fitzgerald's nine took the day.

While a tennis tournament got underway at Windemere, local swimmers and boatmen showed off their skills in a series of races in the waters at the base of Gallop's Hill, from obstacles and relays to underwater swimming and blindfolded dory races.

On Wednesday, every possible mode of transport was made available to the Hull children, who rode to the Nantasket Beach reservation and enjoyed free access to all of the amusements. At Pemberton, the Hull town baseball team took on the soldiers of Fort Revere, defeating them 9-1. After the game, the soldiers gave an exhibition of their drilling techniques, and at night, fireworks lit up the sky.

On Thursday morning, amateur jockeys staked out Manomet Avenue and raced their horses down the middle of the road. Golf, tennis and basketball at the Rockland House kept audiences enthralled.

Friday morning, fencing master Alexander Engel presented an exhibition of his craft on the beach at Kenberma, featuring swords, sabers and foils, and duels on horseback. At 3:30 p.m., the U.S. Life-Savers, under Captain William C. Sparrow, re-enacted a breeches buoy rescue. At 8:00 p.m., the Old Home Week ball at Whitehead signaled the coming end of the celebration.

At 10:30 a.m. on Saturday at Nantasket, the younger crowd participated in "burlesque sports": sack, potato, three-legged, hurry-scurry and greased pig races.

At 1:30 p.m., the Old Home Week grand parade began at Pemberton and headed down Main Street past Elm Square onto Spring Street; it followed Spring to Nantasket Avenue, went over Allerton Hill, through Bayside and Waveland to A Street, turning onto Manomet Avenue, which it followed through Kenberma to Nantasket, up School Street and down Atlantic Avenue to the Hull-Cohasset border on Straits Pond.

The procession included the executive committee of the Hull Old Home Week Association on horseback led by Chief of Police Frank Reynolds; the Working Boys' Band of Boston; the Rockland House automobile, a new attraction that summer, carrying the ladies of Hull; barges drawn by six horses toting young women dressed in the garb of various nations; the Hull fire wagon; the volunteer lifesavers of the Massachusetts Humane Society; a float representing all of the states in the Union, followed by the horse that pulled the surfboat *Nantasket* during the Portland Gale of 1898, as much a recognized hero as the lifesavers; the U.S. Life-Saving Service surfmen of Point Allerton Station; and many more.

After another band concert and yet another baseball game, pitting the Hull team against retired professionals, the ceremonies ended with an illumination.

By the end of the decade, Old Home Week would come to an end in Hull. But it has left behind for us an interesting insight into what residents of the early twentieth century found to be historic about their town, people, events and places that we might otherwise have forgotten today.

Small Town
Big Heart

On average, the world experiences eight thousand mini-earthquakes every single day. With the constant shifting, sliding and colliding of tectonic plates, this number should not really be a surprise. These quakes are not even felt by the average human being. Not until a quake measures a 3.0 or above on the Richter scale do we really feel the earth move, and even then there is little chance of any damage to our structural, manmade world. At 4.0, one might notice knick-knacks on shelves shaking, and at 5.0 slight damage to sturdy structures is possible. Eight hundred moderate quakes, between 5.0 and 5.9, rock the world each year.

Major earthquakes, those registering 7.0 to 7.9 on the scale, are known to occur about eighteen times a year and can cause serious damage. A great earthquake—magnitude 8.0—strikes the world once a year on average, and can cause damage for several hundred miles across.

On Wednesday, April 18, 1906, had the people of San Francisco been allowed to wake up and read the newspapers of their own volition, they might have read a review of tenor Enrico Caruso's performance in *Carmen* at the Mission Opera House the night before. They might have read about the New York Giants baseball team playing the Brooklyn Dodgers in days-old sports news, never dreaming that someday those same Giants would move to their fair city. Or perhaps they'd have caught a note that the Pacific Oto-Ophthalmological Society was in town for a meeting.

Instead, at 5:12 a.m., the earth shook them out of their beds and into a wide-awake nightmare, a version of Hell on Earth.

An earthquake measuring an estimated 7.8 or 7.9 on the Richter scale rocked the San Andreas Fault, with an epicenter just outside of the West Coast's first great city. The quake struck with a force of one gigaton, a unit of explosive force equal to that of one billion tons of TNT.

Nearly three hundred thousand people, three quarters of the population, were instantly homeless. Many fled across the bay to Oakland to escape the fires that broke out in the city, which aided in causing around $400,000,000 in damage. Ruptured natural gas lines fed the fires while ruptured water mains prohibited the fire departments from fighting the fires with any intensity.

The human misery connected with the quake was unparalleled in American history, except, perhaps, by the Galveston hurricane of 1900. Between three thousand and six thousand people died. Thousands more lived in tents near the beach, while still more lived in makeshift relief houses built by the U.S. Army.

Three thousand miles away, the people of Hull heard the cries for help. Five days after the disaster, the selectmen called to order a meeting of citizens interested in helping to alleviate the suffering of the victims of the San Francisco earthquake. Floretta Vining wrote of the meeting in the April 27, 1906 edition of the *Hull Beacon.*

> *Although the weather was very stormy, a goodly number of the public-spirited residents of the town were present, who showed by the spirit with which they entered into the subject that the good people of the old hamlet were, as ever, ready to render assistance to those in distress.*

A committee with Selectman Alfred Galiano as chairman, reporter David Porter Mathews as secretary, and Town Treasurer Clarence Vaughn Nickerson as treasurer formed that night "to canvass the town for subscriptions" of cash to send west. Selectman John Smith, Town Clerk James Jeffrey, Reverend B.L. Duckwall, Sergeant F.F. Lamb from Fort Revere and the coast artillery, police Chief Frank M. Reynolds and other citizens including coal dealer John L. Mitchell, Dr. Walter H. Sturgis, assessor Richard B. Hayes, Gaslavus Falk, William E. Bosworth, storekeeper Charles E. West, Carroll Cleverly and William Gent all pitched in to do their part.

Captain Louis Serovich, a Civil War veteran, lifesaving hero and captain of the Hull-to-Boston steamboat *General Lincoln*, opened his wallet that night and made the first donation of $10. Many others made similar gestures that

The people of Hull had lived through tragedies of their own before, and quite recently, as evidenced by the wreck of the *Abel E. Babcock* during the Portland Gale of 1898, and so felt compelled to help the people of San Francisco when the 1906 earthquake hit.

night, and "the clerk and treasurer were quite busy for a time taking their contributions. The amount subscribed amounted to $100. It is expected that the citizens of the town will bring the total up to over $1,000."

In fact, several South Shore towns went to work to help the people of San Francisco. In Hingham, ex-Governor John Davis Long headed up a meeting to form a committee similar to that of Hull's. In Cohasset, the parishioners of St. Stephen's Episcopal Church raised $500 through their regular collection before they even heard the plea for help from Massachusetts Governor Curtis Guild Jr. In Scituate, funds were raised quietly while the town awaited word from townsfolk known to be in San Francisco at the time of the quake. "Great apprehension is felt by the friends for the possible fate of Mr. and Mrs. Hamilton Welch of this town," read the Scituate column of the April 27 edition of the *Beacon*. "Mr. Welch's last letters home indicated a prolonged stay in San Francisco, with a residence at the Palace hotel." Within days, the Welches wired home news that they had survived and would be fine. Sighs sounded throughout Scituate as the townsfolk raised $520 for disaster relief.

Moving door to door holding out their hands on behalf of the people of San Francisco, the Hull committee members accepted all donations with great thanks. Leona and Leonard Ripley each contributed a dime. Mike Burns of the Oakland House put in five dollars, as did teamster James F. Dowd Jr., fire Chief George Hatchard, E.W. Frost of the Nautilus Inn, doctors William H. Sturgis and William H. Sylvester, Newton Wanzer of the moving company that bore his name and brothers Louis and Joseph Galiano. Fifty-five people contributed two dollars apiece, while seventy others gave half that much.

James Jeffrey, John Smith and Alfred Galiano each contributed ten dollars, as did George A. Smith, proprietor of the popular Smith's Tavern, contractor and former selectman Edward G. Knight and the inimitable Floretta Vining. John L. Mitchell offered twenty-five dollars, hotel man David O. Wade (he of the famous clambakes), gave fifty dollars and the Hull Fireman's Relief Association contributed one hundred dollars.

The big spender, though, was summer resident R.H. Stearns, the department store owner of Boston, who gave $500.

In the end, Hull went over the top with their drive, totaling $1,341.70 in donations forwarded to the firm of Kidder, Peabody, & Company in the city. Hull, with a population of about one thousand citizens, averaged more than a dollar a resident. It wouldn't end the suffering of the people of San Francisco, but it certainly, when coupled with the donations of thousands of other small communities around the country, would go a long way to helping the people of San Francisco back onto their feet after one of the worst natural disasters in American history.

Gala Days

Perhaps with a little more planning, it would have been a success. Maybe if it had been moved to an earlier date and separated from Labor Day weekend, more people would have participated. And, who knows? If somehow the organizers of the first Hull Gala Day in 1908 could have garnered the interest of Floretta Vining's *Hull Beacon*, their idea would have been marketed just a little bit better.

Mr. W.T.A. Fitzgerald, one of the dozens of "prominent men" who spent their summers in Hull each year, suggested the idea of a grand illumination of the beach as early as July that year. His idea grew from simply an end-of-summer celebration of the good life at the seashore to include a series of athletic contests, perhaps in the tradition of the newly revived Olympic Games (the first modern games being held in 1896), to test the mettle of Hull's year-round and summer residents alike.

Living in the shadow of President Theodore Roosevelt, a firm believer in and proponent of "the strenuous life" for every man, woman and child, it would have been hard for Hullonians to ignore the idea.

"Plans for the gala day celebration at Hull on September 5 are not all completed," reported the *Beacon* on August 28, "but thus far water sports, races, ball games, boat races, band concerts and a grand illumination of the summer colony at night have been planned." The illumination would be the first major undertaking of its kind in Hull since 1881.

The September 4 edition of the local paper yielded no mention of the planned activities for the event, but the September 11 edition provided a recap, brief though it was. Unfortunately, the coordinators had allowed the

Gala Days put a focus on outdoor physical activity.

quality of their event to sink below the Vining Line, the moral watermark championed by the *Beacon's* illustrious editor.

> *It certainly is a reflection on those in authority to have permitted such a sorry exhibition of sport (?)as was made on "Hull's Gala Day" in the attempt to catch a poor, tired, frightened, greased pig. Such exhibits are debasing and demoralizing, and are in the category of cock fights, dog fights and other low down so-called sports, which appeal only to a coarse nature. Children should never be permitted to witness such sights, and parents should make this an opportunity to denounce such an exhibition and to teach their little ones a lesson in kindness to our dumb animals.*

Thirty years later, though, W.T.A. Fitzgerald's brainchild had grown to healthy adult status. Even at the lowest depths of the Great Depression, Hull Gala Day stood out as the social event of the summer season in town. Fitzgerald held the title of honorary president in 1937, and the Hull Gala Day committee included a president, nine vice presidents, a secretary, a treasurer and several sub-committees.

Unlike Old Home Week, Gala Days were still taking place in Hull in the 1930s. Yacht races at the end of that decade took place from the new Hull Yacht Club, which once served as the Old Beacon Club at the base of Beacon Street on Allerton Hill.

On Friday night, August 27, 1937, the organizers opened the doors to the Pemberton Inn, one of the last standing reminders of the era of the grand hotels that represented Hull at the turn of the century, for the "Night Before Ball," and the following day, the festivities commenced.

In the 1930s, many of the contests from the early days continued—racing, water sports, baseball games and yacht races—and several new events added to the frivolity at the Bayside fields. Those folks who could not catch a pop fly or run in a three-legged race could dance, play quoits (a form of ring toss) and compete in the summer-long tennis tournaments organized by Joe Conway, the finals of which were held on Hull Gala Day.

For the kids, Punch and Judy shows made them laugh, fireworks sparkled in their eyes and ponies gladly carried them on their backs. The events also included picture shows at the Bayside Theatre, a band concert and a parade.

Editor Herb Gordon of the *Hull Times* gave Hull Gala Day a much better review than did the irrepressible Floretta Vining before him. But then, it seems, he had much more with which to work. He wrote of the event in his August 26, 1937 editorial.

Originated by the Hon. W.T.A. Fitzgerald and his associates, the Gala Day program has grown increasingly popular with each passing year, until it is now recognized as one of the outstanding social functions of its kind on the Atlantic Coast...

Gala Day has produced many public benefits during its steady progress. Besides the advantages of healthy competition, inculcating the principles of sportsmanship in the great number of youngsters, as well as adults who enjoy participation in one or more of the various games on the program, it has at the same time developed a splendid spirit of good-will, friendship and civic pride among the entire population.

Hull Gala Day continued as an annual event into the 1960s, but eventually faded away. The day always brought out the joy of the season for all, but with it the twinge of sadness that yet another summer had come to an end.

Childe Harold

Hal Janvrin's mother could only hope that her son got the nickname "Childe Harold" for his youthful looks and the fact that he shared the first name of the main character in Lord Byron's epic poem "Childe Harold's Pilgrimage," and nothing else. Judging by his appearance in the accompanying photos from the National Baseball Hall of Fame Library, that's a pretty safe bet, especially as Janvrin gained the epithet after joining the Boston Red Sox, fresh out of high school in 1911.

Lord Byron's semi-autobiographical poem, partially written both before and after his self-imposed exile from England on April 25, 1816, tells the story of the world travels of a supposedly fictitious wayward English youth. After partaking of a two-year visit to lands as distant as Portugal, Spain and Greece, Byron returned to London in 1811 "with his head full of romantic notions," and began writing both "Childe Harold" and his Oriental tales, works which brought him instant and unexpected popularity. On January 2, 1815, he married a Miss Milbanke; within a year she left him, taking their newborn daughter with her. Paul Elmer More writes in *The Complete Poetical Works of Byron*, "Into the causes and mysteries of the divorce we may not enter. Byron was wild and his wife was a prude; it would seem that nothing more should need be said." The British public sided with the Lady Byron, and the poet left his native land never to see England again.

As for Childe Harold himself, Byron introduced him thusly:

> *Whilome in Albion's isle there dwelt a youth,*
> *Who ne in virtues ways did take delight;*

But spent his days in riot most uncouth,
And vex'd with mirth the drowsy ear of Night.
Ah me! in sooth he was a shameless wight,
Sore given to revel and ungodly glee;
Few earthly things found favour in his sight
Save concubines and carnal companie,
And flaunting wassailers of high and low degree.

Mrs. Janvrin could only pray it was her son's youthful looks.

A summer resident of Hull, Hal Janvrin first appeared in the *Hull Beacon* as a schoolboy baseball star, albeit as just one of the starting nine competing in an all-star game pulled together as part of the town's 1910 Gala Days celebration. The August 12, 1910 edition of the *Beacon* reported on the game.

Following the field sports will come the chief event of the day, the ball game between the "Brookline Gyms," one of the fastest amateur organizations in New England, and a picked nine representing the summer residents of Allerton. Charlie McLaughlin, captain of next year's Harvard varsity nine, his brother Jim, who played centre field on the Yale freshman team this year, Harold Janvrin of the English high school, Tommy Boles, the Phillips Andover star shortstop, Joe Kennedy of Harvard, Al Dickenshied, "Fish" Gallagher of the Roger Wolcotts, and other young interscholastic cracks will compose the Bayside team, and silver medals will be awarded the winners. James A. Gallivan has charge of this event and promises a closely contested match.

No other player on the local all-star team would ever go pro. First baseman Joe Kennedy of Harvard, though, did have a son grow up to be president of the United States.

We may never know the result of the game, as the *Beacon* did not feel it necessary to print it the next week. One of the silver medals surfaced in Hull in the late 1990s, though, purchased by a Hull resident. Was it ever pinned on the chest of the father of an American president or a Red Sox infielder? The answer is seemingly lost in time.

Born on August 27, 1892, in Haverhill, Massachusetts, Hal Janvrin joined the Red Sox for nine games in 1911, playing both first and third base. After spending the 1912 season in the minor leagues, he rejoined the Sox in 1913, establishing himself as a major league-caliber player, although he would

Hal Janvrin set major league records while playing with the Boston Red Sox. *Courtesy Baseball Hall of Fame Library, Cooperstown, New York.*

never earn himself a steady starting job. Janvrin hit a career-high three home runs that year, which also represented half of his career total of six, tying a major league record on October 4 that stands today by hitting two inside-the-park jobs in the same game. The record has been duplicated on several occasions, the last time ironically being exactly seventy-three years to the day after Janvrin's feat, on October 4, 1986. Even more ironic is the fact that the man to do it on that day was also a Massachusetts native, Minnesota Twins shortstop Greg Gagne of Fall River.

In 1914, Childe Harold found his way into a career-high 143 games, playing first, second, third and shortstop, as well as having a front row seat for the beginning of the career of the man who is still one of the most prolific home run hitters of all time, rookie pitcher and at least one-time

Even with wrinkles around his eyes, Hal Janvrin still showed the youthful looks that earned him the nickname "Childe Harold." *Courtesy Baseball Hall of Fame Library, Cooperstown, New York.*

visitor to Hull George Herman "Babe" Ruth. That year would also be the only year that Hal Janvrin would hit more home runs than the Babe. He had one. The Babe had none.

The following year proved to be a magical one for the Sox, as they won the World Series after an interminable wait of three years since their last championship. Led by future Hall of Fame outfielders Harry Hooper and Tris "The Grey Eagle" Speaker and under the management of "Wild" Bill Carrigan, the Sox, after taking the pennant without playing a full schedule (they played three games less than the Detroit Tigers, but had one more win at the end of the season), ran over the Philadelphia Phillies four games to one. Both Janvrin and Ruth rode the bench during the series. On July 2, the Sox had acquired second baseman Jack Barry from Connie Mack's Philadelphia Athletics, gambling in mid-season that his four years of World Series experience (1910–14) would come in handy. Ruth, as the team's third starter, won eighteen games during the regular season, but was bypassed for a three-man rotation of "Rube" Foster, Ernie Shore and Dutch Leonard. Ruth and Janvrin each had one at bat in the Series, neither one getting a hit.

Another member of the Sox that sat out the series, submarine-throwing rookie Carl "Sub" Mays, led the team in saves that year with seven. Although he would eventually win more than two hundred games with the Red Sox, New York Yankees, Cincinnati Reds and New York Giants, he will forever be known as the only man to kill an opposing player with a pitched ball in a major league game. On August 16, 1920, in the fifth inning of a game with the Cleveland Indians, Mays, then with the Yankees, threw a brush back pitch at Cleveland shortstop and fellow Kentuckian Ray Chapman. The batter, leaning over ready to bunt, did not react in time, and the ball struck him square in the left temple, sending a sickening cracking sound through the Polo Grounds. Chapman sank to his knees, staring blankly, before collapsing. Mays called the umpire to the mound to show him a scuff on the ball, his excuse for the bad pitch. He later would also state that the ball was wet from the rain that had fallen through the first few innings. He then complained that Chapman was faking an injury to get a free base. The following day, the twenty-nine-year old Chapman died of a fractured skull. For a full account of the story, see Mike Sowell's *The Pitch That Killed*.

In 1916, Hal Janvrin became one of the few players that was ever able to claim that he was a two-time Boston Red Sox World Series champion. Batting leadoff as the team's starting second baseman, he set another major league record still holding strong today, recording twenty-three at-bats in the five game World Series, a total matched only twice, by Joe Moore of the Giants in 1937 and Bobby Richardson of the Yankees in 1961. The series—which started just a day after German U-boats sank six ships off Nantucket—went just five games, with the Sox taking out the Brooklyn Dodgers four games to one. The Sox won the series despite jettisoning both Tris Speaker and star pitcher "Smoky" Joe Wood after salary disputes in the off-season. After the series, owner Joe Lannin (a former Hull hotel owner) announced that he would sell the team.

Hal Janvrin's star began to fade after the 1916 season. He played only fifty-five games in 1917 and missed the entire Red Sox 1918 World Series Championship season, signing up for armed service on December 17, 1917, the eleventh member of the team to leave for World War I, according to Ty Waterman and Mel Springer's *The Year the Red Sox Won the World Series*. On January 17, 1919, just two months after the end of the war, the Sox traded him to the Washington Senators with cash in exchange for veteran catcher and Cambridge native Eddie Ainsmith (who was traded within twenty-four hours to the Detroit Tigers) and pitcher George "Pea Soup" Dumont. Just eight months later, on September 10, the St. Louis Cardinals picked up Janvrin on waivers. On June 18, 1921, the Cardinals traded Janvrin and well-traveled pitcher Ferdie Schupp to the Brooklyn Dodgers for Jeff Pfeffer, the younger brother of Big Jeff Pfeffer. Apparently, the Illinois Pfeffers weren't very creative.

In ten years of big league service, Hal Janvrin played in 756 games, batting .232 with 515 hits and 79 stolen bases. He played alongside Hall of Famers, won two World Series and set two major league records. And at one time, he may have worn a silver medal for an exhibition game played in Hull.

The day he retired, Hal Janvrin, ultimately linked with Lord Byron's hero, may have taken a moment to reflect on the words with which the poet ended his work:

> *My task is done—my song has ceased—my theme*
> *Has died into an echo; it is fit*
> *The spell should break of this protracted dream.*
> *The torch shall be extinguish'd which hath lit*
> *My midnight lamp—and what is writ,—*
> *Would it were worthier! but I am not now*
> *That which I have been—and my visions flit*
> *Less palpably before me—and the glow*
> *Which in my spirit dwelt is fluttering, fain, and low.*

Hal Janvrin, Hull summer resident and Red Sox hero, died in Boston on March 1, 1962.

A Bit of Hull History
Heads to Sea

The opening of the Cape Cod Canal in 1914 solved a number of problems for Boston merchants hoping to safely ship their products to all points south along the East Coast.

United States Life-Saving Service records indicate that between 1875 and 1903, no fewer than 687 ships met with disaster on the shores between Monomoy and Provincetown, leaving at least 105 people dead.

The passage through the canal meant avoiding the rips and shoals of the Outer Cape and sidestepping the thick, heavy fog that envelops the waters off Chatham for an average 130 days each year.

Yet, while solving many problems, the canal created an unusual situation for the residents of the community of Buzzards Bay. The canal cut them off from most of the community's churches. The churches ended up on the south side, while most of the parishioners remained on the north side. It now took about four hours to get to the Sunday services.

On March 27, 1938, the Episcopalian residents of Buzzards Bay began regular Sunday services in Red Men's Hall, a local lodge, with lay readers and with archdeacons serving as spiritual leaders. They hoped someday to have their own church, but didn't quite know how to go about building one.

During these years a young clergyman, Reverend John Samuel Stephenson, became enamored of the Episcopal community in Buzzards Bay. Having studied in Philadelphia, Father Steve, as he will forever

A church that once stood in Hull is now a mainstay of the Buzzards Bay community, St. Peter's on the Canal. *Courtesy of author.*

affectionately be known, spent summers in the little village with his sister, who owned a home there.

By 1944, his heart was in Buzzards Bay for good. That year he accepted a missionary post, running both the St. Peter's parish in Buzzards Bay and that of St. John's in Sandwich.

He and his wife Carolyn immediately began their quest to build a church. Knowing that the parishioners could never raise enough money on their own, they sought outside help.

Carolyn wrote to the *Vox Pop* radio program, a popular quiz and interview show that aired on CBS Radio every Monday night (brought to you by Bromo Seltzer). Parks Johnson and Warren Hull came down and broadcast their show live one night from Buzzards Bay, allowing Father Steve to send out a plea for help across the nation. They returned a year later to promote the Father's "Teen Town" youth program, and the donations came rolling in. By the spring of 1947, the building appropriation fund totaled around $6,000. But the most generous gift of all was yet to come.

Forty-five miles up the coast, in another seaside community known as Hull, sat the unused forty-five-year-old Episcopal Church of Our Savior, on the corner of N Street and Nantasket Avenue, near the old Bayside train station. The Episcopalians in Hull negotiated a price with Father Steve and told him he could have the church, provided he paid the moving expenses.

Father Steve had always been a resourceful man. He did whatever he could to support his family, whether it was helping out on Sumner Towne's tuna boat or playing piano at the King Midas Diner. One year he ran his own scallop boat, hiring three Italian women to shuck for him, delighting as they sang old Italian songs in beautiful harmony. So it came as no surprise when he found a way to get the church from Hull to Buzzards Bay on short money.

Finding out it would be too expensive to move it over land, Father Steve consulted a friend in the moving business who said it would be plausible to move it by sea. By May of 1947, all of the preparations were made and an army barge sat on Nantasket Beach awaiting cargo.

The church stood seventy feet long by forty-five feet wide and weighed around seventy tons, or one hundred and forty thousand pounds (it has since been lengthened). The movers lifted it off its foundation and onto trucks that then drove a hundred yards down the sandy road and onto the beach. The steeple had to be removed for the church to pass under the power lines, although the original bell did make the trip.

The trucks struggled once on the beach and boards had to be placed under the tires more than once for added traction. The tugboat *Bounty* pulled the barge out to sea, and onward they went, covering sixty nautical miles to Buzzards Bay.

The journey was not an easy one. Bad weather sent the tug scurrying for shelter for a few days, and once down in Cape Cod Bay a towline snapped, almost causing the barge and tug to collide. Yet the church did reach land safely as cheering townsfolk lined the shore to welcome their "little church that came in on the tide."

Without the aid of heavy moving equipment, Father Steve again had to brainstorm. In the end, the never-say-die parishioners resorted to wooden rollers and ropes to move their new church to its final location.

The last mile proved to be the toughest one of the journey. The head of the local state police barracks called a halt to the rolling church and explained to Father Steve that he could not issue a permit to move a church across a state highway, now Main Street. On this point he was adamant. As the dejected minister turned to leave, the chief quietly explained to him that, in a few months' time, he and the rest of the state police would be out of town at a convention for four or five hours on a certain date. With a wink, he ended the discussion. That date came and went, and no state policeman ever asked how the little church crossed the road.

St. Peter's Church-on-the-Canal, as it was named for the biblical fisherman, has undergone many changes in the past sixty years. Edgar Johnson, one of the original parishioners, has seen them all.

Two parish halls have been added, buildings taken from Otis Air Force Base. In 1964 a new steeple replaced the one left behind in Hull, and, in 1966, the parish purchased the adjacent properties and landscaped them. Around that time, Carolyn Stephenson helped set up St. Peter's Exchange, a building used to recycle clothing and household goods for the community.

The interior of the church has been almost completely refurbished over the years. Reflecting its patron saint, the church has a nautical theme. While on a four-year stay in Buffalo, New York, Father Steve met and befriended three talented woodcarvers, whom he convinced to help out the St. Peter's parish. Edgar Johnson, who remembers the original pews as "the most uncomfortable things you ever wanted to sit on," smiled when the new ones arrived from Buffalo. They are now set up in the church with alternating hand-carved anchors and arks facing the aisle.

The parish removed a large westward-facing window from behind the altar, as the setting sun often caused problems for the congregation's eyes. They installed eight new plate-glass windows, four along each side of the church, all of which depict some aspect of the life of the fisherman apostle.

Father Steve did return to his parish and preached there until his retirement. Seventeen years after that he passed away, one day after making a parochial call on a couple who were members of the church.

Change

It's July 4, 1905. You're a passenger on the *Mayflower*, one of the palatial steamers on the Boston-to-Hull run. You've managed to escape work in the city for the day and have opted to beat the heat by enjoying the cool ocean breezes of Nantasket Beach. Before stepping onto the bustling pier at the steamboat landing you take one last peek at one of Frederick Law Olmstead's latest creations, a landscaped park on the two hills of the old Brewer family farm in Hingham. Rows of saplings line carefully laid-out roads that fit the natural contours of the hills, and someone has spread a blanket for a picnic, enjoying the view from the other side of the Weir River.

On the wharf you hold closely to your wallet, as you've heard horror stories of pickpockets and thieves that do their best work preying upon unsuspecting first-time visitors to the beach. Before you can cross to the sand and rolling surf you're accosted by a row of vendors hawking everything from peanuts to photography. You quickstep past the new Metropolitan Park Commission's lock-up, dodge one of the open-air electrics for which Nantasket is famous and head for the entrance to the beach through the Hotel Nantasket. The desire to stop for some refreshment almost pulls you into the Rockland Café, but your need to get into the salt water is even stronger. You head for the bathhouse at the base of Atlantic Hill, all the while marveling at the beauty of the ever-expanding Atlantic House hotel, wondering if you'll ever have enough money to spend the night in one of its rooms. You even contemplate checking out the new big thing at the beach, a place called Paragon Park, just opened about a month ago.

View from the Depot, Nantasket Beach, Mass.

Stepping ashore at Nantasket Steamboat Wharf in 1905, one wandered past Peanut Row and headed for the Nantasket Hotel, its boardwalk, bandstand and the beach.

You rent your wool bathing suit and head for the water, playing on the beach until the last of the Independence Day fireworks have burst.

Fast forward. It's July 4, 1955. You've decided to escape the heat of the city with a trip down to Nantasket Beach. As you pass World's End, you smile at the beauty of the tree-lined walkways and watch as great egrets feed among the marsh grasses. Glancing to the right as your boat pulls into the old Nantasket Steamboat Wharf you spy the venerable steamboat *Mayflower*, high and dry after the big fire of 1929. If all goes well, you'll be catching the last boat back to the city after seeing a show in the famous "showboat," a singer, perhaps, or a ventriloquist. The boat sits on the edge of George Washington Boulevard, laid out in 1932 on the two hundredth anniversary of the birth of the first president of the United States. The smell from the new Nantasket Lobster Pound arrives aboard before the lines are tied to the dock.

As soon as you step off the boat the sound hits you. You cross the street and head for Paragon Park, New England's world fair, the Massachusetts answer to Coney Island for the past fifty years. For just a few dollars you can ride the famous giant coaster, munch on some saltwater taffy and play a few games of chance. Nantasket Avenue is packed with automobiles and people alike. The old train bed is gone, having been pulled up eighteen years ago.

Vendors on Peanut Row sold everything from fruit…

You head for the bathhouse to grab a bathing suit and towel and relax on the beach, listening for the sounds of a live band at the bandstand. You stay until the last of the Independence Day fireworks have burst in the sky.

Fast-forward one more time. It's July 4, 2005, and you've had enough of the heat in the city. You catch a ride on a friend's boat down the Weir River to the ancient Nantasket Steamboat Wharf. The steamboats don't run here anymore, as the Weir River area where it approaches the wharf has been designated as an area of critical environmental concern by the state of Massachusetts. The spectacular view of World's End Reservation catches your eye and you realize that Frederick Law Olmstead's vision of 1893 has stood the test of time. Glancing to the right you see that the space where the old steamer *Mayflower* once sat is empty, the boat having burned to the ground in 1979. The old steamboat terminal is gone, too. You've even heard rumor that a recent Hull town manager fell through the floor and broke an arm during an inspection before it was demolished. But the area around the pier is alive with activity, as the town of Hull has called for the dredging of forty new transient slips for boaters and is reviewing bids for new residential and retail buildings. The smell of

...to soda.

lobster coming from Jake's Seafood Restaurant hits you before the boat pulls into the wharf.

Crossing the street you see kids at play in the old Paragon Park parking lot in a street hockey rink. High-rise condominiums have replaced the vertical space once occupied by the roller coaster that you hear is now somewhere in Maryland, Paragon Park having closed in 1985 after eighty years of lighting up the night sky. As you look up at the condos and imagine the view from inside, you feel that their residents must be some of the luckiest people in the world.

The sounds of the Paragon Carousel's Wurlitzer military band organ, moved with the rest of the ride and its building down the street when the park closed, still tickle the ear as they did in the thirties when it first arrived in Hull, a few years after the merry-go-round had already been in place. The whirling horses, some in bad repair, others newly refurbished, still delight children of all ages. The old train station now houses an ice cream store. Across the street, the state has rebuilt the Bernie King Pavilion, named for the longtime bandleader who became a favorite of the locals.

The *Mayflower* was the last of the steamers standing in Hull, saved from the 1929 fire and later used as a nightclub.

Looking north up Nantasket Avenue past the old Massachusetts state police's recently closed station you see the new state bathhouse and the beautiful new Clarion Hotel. Looking south to Atlantic Hill you spy the condominiums that stand where the old Atlantic House hotel once rested. Crossing the street you head for the beach, stepping past a Department of Conservation work crew tidying up the flowerbeds that line the beach parking lots. Relaxing in the sand and surf until nightfall, you watch the last of the Independence Day fireworks along the far-off line of the North Shore.

Yes, the face of Nantasket Beach is changing again. Sadly, some landmarks—like the old Bernie King Pavilion, the last vestige of the Hotel Nantasket and the steamboat terminal building, famous (or infamous, as it may be) as a spot where an American president once relieved himself—are on the way out, while new buildings like the new pavilion and the Clarion mark a new era for Nantasket Beach. The fact remains, though, that just as a traveler in 1905 might not recognize much on his way from the steamboat wharf to the beach today, a visitor from 2005 following the same route in 2105 will have the same problems.

Sometimes in the face of the best-intentioned attempts at historic preservation, time and the elements simply win, and it's up to a town to shift gears and follow the best course for the community's economic future. Some businesses survive and thrive for years, while others come and go quickly. Buildings adaptable for reuse stand a better chance of remaining intact with new tenants as circumstances dictate, while others crumble. But through it all, the attraction of the sand and surf remains.

If you're a longtime resident of Hull, think back on the changes that have taken place at Nantasket Beach in your lifetime. If you're a first-time visitor to Hull, be sure to buy some film and snap a few photographs. Things move fast on Nantasket Beach, and it may not look the same the next time you come to town.

But if that beach could speak, what stories it would tell of Old Nantasket.

Bibliography

Baker, William A. *A History of the Boston Marine Society 1742–1967*. Boston, MA: Boston Marine Society, 1968.

Bergan, William M. *Old Nantasket*. North Quincy, MA: Christopher Publishing House, 1968.

Bigelow, E. Victor. *A Narrative History of the Town of Cohasset*. Cohasset, MA: The Committee on Town History, 1898.

Biographical Review, Volume XVII, Containing Life Sketches of Leading Citizens of Plymouth County, Massachusetts. Boston: Biographical Review Publishing, 1897.

Biographical Review, Volume XXVII, Containing Life Sketches of Leading Citizens of Middlesex County, Massachusetts. Boston: Biographical Review Publishing, 1898.

History of the Town of Hingham, Massachusetts. Hingham, MA: Town of Hingham, 1893.

Chidsey, Donald Barr. *John the Great: The Times and Life of a Remarkable American, John L. Sullivan*. Garden City, NY: Doubleday, Doran and Co., 1942.

Clymer, Floyd. *Treasury of Early American Automobiles, 1877–1925*. New York: McGraw-Hill, 1950.

Crabb, Richard. *Birth of a Giant: The Men and Incidents that Gave America the Motorcar.* Philadelphia: Chilton Book Co., 1969.

Deane, Samuel. *History of Scituate, Massachusetts, from its First Settlement to 1831.* Boston: J. Loring, 1831.

Dibble, R.F. *John L. Sullivan.* Boston: Little, Brown and Company, 1925.

Digges, Jeremiah. *Cape Cod Pilot.* Provincetown, MA: Modern Pilgrim Press, 1937.

Glidden, Charles. "To the Arctic Circle in a Motor Car," *New England Magazine,* January 1904.

Homer, James Lloyd. *Notes on the Sea-Shore, or, Random Sketches.* Boston: Redding & Co., 1848.

Hull Beacon, 1897–1920. On microfilm at the Hull Public Library.

Hull Times, 1930–present.

Hurd, D. Hamilton, comp. *History of Plymouth County, Massachusetts.* Philadelphia: J.W. Lewis & Co., 1884.

Kurlansky, Mark. *Cod: A Biography of the Fish that Changed the World.* New York: Walker and Company, 1997.

Labaree, Benjamin Woods. *The Boston Tea Party.* Boston: Northeastern University Press, 1979.

Moore, John. "History of Hull," serialized in the *Hull Beacon,* 1900-1901.

More, Paul Elmer, ed. *The Complete Poetical Works of Byron.* Boston: Houghton-Mifflin, 1933.

O'Reilly, John Boyle. *Ethics of Boxing and Manly Sport.* Boston: Ticknor and Company, 1888.

Roche, James Jeffrey. *Life of John Boyle O'Reilly.* New York: Cassell Publishing Company, 1891.

Bibliography

Russell, Francis T. *The Knave of Boston and Other Ambiguous Massachusetts Characters.* Boston: Quinlan Press, 1987.

Sears, Stephen W. *The American Heritage History of the Automobile in America.* New York: Simon and Schuster, 1977.

Sowell, Mike. *The Pitch That Killed.* New York: Macmillan, 1989.

Tager, Jack and John W. Ifkovic, eds. *Massachusetts in the Gilded Age.* Amherst, MA: University of Massachusetts Press, 1985.

Thompson, Elroy S. *History of Plymouth, Norfolk and Barnstable Counties, Massachusetts.* 3 vols. New York: Lewis Historical Publishing Co., 1928.

Turner, Robert I. "History of the Catholic Church in Hull." Unpublished manuscript.

Waterman, Ty and Mel Springer. *The Year the Red Sox Won the World Series.* Boston: Northeastern University Press, 1999.

About the Author

John Galluzzo is president of the Fort Revere Park & Preservation Society and a longtime contributor of history articles to the *Hull Times*. He has previously authored fourteen books on local and national history, including two on Hull with his friends at the Committee for the Preservation for Hull's History. *The Golden Age of Hull* is his second title with The History Press.

Visit us at
www.historypress.com